WHAT PEOPLE ARE SAYING ABOUT

GO! SMELL THE FLOWERS

The Jimbo I know from Dubai is probably not going to be the flower smeller that I know but someone else I do not know - I hope! Enjoy the book that details this journey of change flowers smellers.
Sir Ian Botham.

Life is to short not to GO! Smell the flowers and this book is a great place to inspire change and to start living the life you want. **Lee Sharpe**, ex Man united and England footballer now a T.V pundit and reality T.V regular.

A great his n her book - 2 perspectives on the same experience makes for an interesting read with a twist at the end. My wife and I raced to read this book every day!
Steve Thompson M.B.E, former Rugby Union player for London Wasps, England and the British & Irish Lions.

A enlightening story of inspiration that encourages get up and GO!
Carly Booth, Professional golfer and winner of the 2012 Ladies Scottish Open.

This book will make you laugh, possibly even cry and give you the strength and courage to step into your greatness. GO! For it.
Katherine Roberts, Founder and President: Yoga for golfers.

T0308547

Go!
Smell the Flowers

One Journey, Many Discoveries

Go!
Smell the Flowers

One Journey, Many Discoveries

Jim and Emma Wheat

BOOKS

Winchester, UK
Washington, USA

First published by O-Books, 2013
O-Books is an imprint of John Hunt Publishing Ltd., Laurel House, Station Approach,
Alresford, Hants, SO24 9JH, UK
office1@jhpbooks.net
www.johnhuntpublishing.com

For distributor details and how to order please visit the 'Ordering' section on our website.

Design: Stuart Davies

Printed in the USA by Edwards Brothers Malloy

We operate a distinctive and ethical publishing philosophy in all
areas of our business, from our global network of authors to
production and worldwide distribution.

CONTENTS

Acknowledgements

We would like to thank...

Jo Parfitt and her Book Cooks for making our 'his n her' scripts come together and flow into what you are about to read.

Our panel of readers who took the time to read the raw form of this book and give us the honest feedback we needed. Your thoughts and honesty were greatly appreciated.

And finally, particular thanks to Allan and Barbara Pease, whose guidance throughout the writing process was deeply appreciated..

GO! Smell the flowers, while you still can.

One journey, many discoveries.

'You are not here merely to make a living. You are here to enable the world to live more amply, with greater vision, and with a finer spirit of hope and achievement. You are here to enrich the world. You impoverish yourself if you forget this errand.'
Woodrow Wilson

Foreword

Allan and Barbara Pease
International Authors Extraordinaire

Allan

Our first contact with Jim & Emma came when a magazine approached us to give advice to two aspiring young authors and become their long-distance mentors. Despite our hectic schedule with worldwide speaking engagements and book PR tours, plus a busy family life, we agreed to share what we had learned on the rocky road to writing a bestseller. Embarking on writing a book is one thing, but to do a 'his n hers' version of the same story is another. Jim & Emma have successfully managed this whilst combining a wonderful love story into a journey of self discovery and a fantastic example of the law of attraction.

Barbara

After setting the British tabloids on fire with our study into women's difficulties with reverse parking we started on our own journey of the 'his n her' differences. Our own humorous insights into relationships between men and women will give readers a useful insight into the love story that Jim & Emma have written.

Allan

GO! Smell the flowers is both thought provoking and entertaining whilst capturing the zest for life these remarkable people have. Having recovered from cancer while continuing my world tour and writing 14 bestselling books - over 20 million copies in 140 countries - I'm a person who has smelt many flowers. My survival and success came from deciding what I wanted from my life and making a step-by-step plan of action and following through on my goals. Whether you are successful or floating around like a ship without a rudder GO! Smell the flowers will provide you with the inspiration to make it happen.

Barbara

GO! Smell the flowers is a well-timed breath of fresh air in a time when countless people are questioning their own existence.

It has been a wonderful experience being Jim & Emma's long-distance mentors as they inspire countless others around the world. Look no further and as Jim & Emma say "GO! Smell the flowers, while you still can!"

Allan and Barbara Pease
www.peaseinternational.com

How to use this book

GO! Smell the flowers is our his 'n' hers account of the same journey through different eyes. Our book of 'one journey, many discoveries' is written as an account of travel, of change and, will we hope, serve as an inspiration for you, the reader.

Throughout the book there are questions that you are free to ignore, read or think about. There are also quotations that are designed to encapsulate the relevant piece of writing or put a broader slant on our experiences.

We want to give you the opportunity to dig deep and get more from this book than just reading the story – if that is what you want ... it is your choice.

These are the sub-headings you will find throughout the text to identify questions, reflections, action and information.

GO! THINK - Questions designed to make you think, dig deep and call upon your experiences to date.

GO! READ - Books we enjoyed reading and wanted to share with you.

GO! Do it! – Our summary at the end of each chapter.

GO! DISCOVER – A brief summary in the Appendix to share some of our discoveries.

Enjoy it and remember:
Go! Smell the flowers along the way.

Prologue

Dubai – the present day

> Change is the law of life. and those who look only to the past
> or present are certain to miss the future.
> John F Kennedy

As we stand arm in arm in our Sheik Zayed Road apartment, a
wisp of sandalwood incense smoke softens the view. Despite the
14 lanes of traffic and the countless towering sky cranes
stretching up above the dusty Dubai skyline an amazing feeling
of wellbeing and contentment floods over us.

"Wake up!" You think.

Or is it "Oh come on, pass me the bucket"?

"You're dreaming."

Well, it is no dream. This has become our reality and one that
we never imagined we'd find.

What follows is our humble story of change and how we
arrived at our present state of mind having quit the rat race
through gritted teeth to leave Dubai and put our lives into
perspective. Before we go headlong into our journey allow us to
rewind back and explain how we both ended up in Dubai in the
first place.

Jim's World

Up until September 2002 I had been living in a terraced house in
Chester in the north of England. My reason to be was selling
chemicals. Not just any old chemicals you understand but the
finest on earth that can be added to concrete on all manner of
projects. I spent my working week travelling the country, eating
at truck stops and battling to keep sales figures up and my
waistline down.

I was working in a quiet market that permitted plenty of thinking time, time to plan, time to dream. My dream was to get away from this relentless chemical treadmill and be posted abroad, preferably somewhere warm and busy - on another treadmill. Driving in circles from one forced sales call to another around rain-soaked Manchester was rapidly losing its appeal.

Then a sudden break in the clouds appeared as I learned that there was an opening, an opportunity. It was to head up the marketing team over in Dubai - the dream of all expat postings. Post 9/11 most of my friends and colleagues thought I was mad to even consider going off to weave my chemical-enhanced magic in a land they perceived to be riddled with booby traps and nightclub bombings. But I knew what I felt about it in a heartbeat despite what CNN led me to believe.

The lads at the local pub, rugby and golf club shouted me up a farewell curry to see me on my way. With a Chicken Chilli Balti in my belly and eight pints of Guinness Extra Cold I left with the hope that these social essentials would be available in the United Arab Emirates.

I arrived in the October, with the remnants of yet another hangover but this time in a temperature of 35 degrees C and 80 per cent humidity. Back then, it was just me, an empty air-conditioned company flat, a private gym, sauna and rooftop pool. The week after arriving I celebrated my 31st birthday, alone, with a slice of cake from Spinney's supermarket decorated with a solitary blue candle.

I soon settled into the Dubai way of life however, where unlike the UK, the construction boom was rapidly gaining momentum; already the highest producer of concrete per head of population in the world. This city was on the up, both proverbially and physically, and so too were the thousands of people from all over the world expatriating to the place. In fact over 120 nationalities have now chosen to call Dubai home and the line up of customers in almost any coffee shop in town would confirm this where you will normally find a fair scattering of Brits amongst other latte drinking South Africans, Lebanese, Egyptians and French. Coffee is strictly off limits to me now but more of that later, or should that be latte?

Projects in Dubai provided monthly sales figures equivalent to 12 months' worth back in the UK without the grey bureaucracy that the industry faced at home. The audacity of the city's rulers in their attempt to make it the global hub for business and tourism when the spoils of oil run out around 2020 was breathtaking. Growing out of the once-blue Arabian waters, for example, was The World, an ambitious project consisting of a series of 200 man-made islands shaped to form the world map as the dredgers spewed out Palm Island further on up the coast.

After just three years in Dubai, we had busted all budgets. The once desert hardship posting was now the place to be and a global brand in its own right. A century ago, it was a fishing village whose coral-and-gypsum huts housed Bedouin traders and pearl divers. Now the only pearls noticeable were the ones dripping off the necks of the bored expat wives of Jumeirah. Today the merchants had gone international and science-fiction skyscrapers stood alongside the mosques and wind towers of Old Dubai.

My 'new' life in Dubai differed from that in England in many ways but the grass wasn't always greener. I had traded in my face-to-face client contact back in the UK for a one-on-one relationship with my computer keyboard where my daily efforts were spent justifying, defending and protecting both my importance and my department and, I recognised, ultimately made little difference to whether the graphs went up or down on those PowerPoint charts. In truth it was the market that dictated our meteoric rise and we were the concrete answer to everything because we were smack bang in the middle of the Disneyland market of Dubai – not because I was some strategic whizz kid.

I could not fool myself any longer. My patience was running

out along with the oil reserves. The rulers of the Gulf States wisely recognised this (the oil thing not my patience) and decided to give it their best shot by turning their homeland into a tourist destination. 'Build and they will come,' they said. They built and people were still coming as the construction orgasm continued.

Granted, the relationships the team built up with their customer base, the level of service we offered and our after sales and technical support all played their part; but the year-on-year market growth outweighed all these attributes. But my role on the management team was, in truth, down to my skill of ensuring that I was at my keyboard from 08:00 to 17:30, five days a week.

"What exactly *is* it that you do?" I was asked from time to time, largely by the field sales blokes.

"Become the marketing manager and you'll find out," I'd reply with varying degrees of defensiveness.

"It's far more than the T-shirt and mugs department you know," became my regular reply.

What I *did* do was emails. My job was emails. I had become adept at emails. I'd even progressed from two-finger typing to almost three as I dared to allow my thumb to drop onto the space bar from time to time.

My cleverness in responding to emails and keeping an empty inbox were my only means of bringing my 'to-do' list down to zero and that justified my return home from a 'good day's work'. I *was* marketing. I was clever too, but something in my life was seriously missing.

Maybe I had made a mistake coming to Dubai after all.

Emma's World

I arrived in Sharjah, a little-known Emirate that borders Dubai, in August 1996 with my husband, Charlie. Life in the UK had lost its charm, house prices had risen steeply and salaries were not keeping pace. With Charlie's future not looking bright after a round of redundancies at the bank in which he worked, we decided not to hang around to learn his fate but to make a move to a more exciting life.

I was a trained primary school teacher and, rather dramatically, accepted a teaching post in Sharjah, 'somewhere in the Middle East', which I had seen advertised in the Times Educational Supplement. I had no idea what to expect but our thinking was that the move would pay off our mortgage within ten years, enabling us to get the things we had always wanted in life. As one of the more traditional seven Emirates, the Sharjah Creek was a world I had never seen. It was lined with old buildings and rickety wooden dhows, piled high with a brightly coloured plastic-wrapped cargo that was then unloaded by a handful of exhausted ship-hands after an arduous journey across the Indian ocean to the Gulf of Arabia. This, together with the old souk area, its long narrow alley ways and the humid air thick with aromatic spices, conjured up old oil paintings of the Arabia I had often seen as a child.

Despite the overwhelming immersion into Arabic culture, the move, however, didn't quite prove to be the golden ticket we had expected. We had traded in a small, detached, three-bedroom Wimpey house with a nice garden and garage in the UK and were now living in a tiny one-bedroom apartment in a grey cement block, overlooking a busy side street. My job was not as I had expected either. Due to the language barrier, it turned out to be more babysitting than teaching and with little parental interest, before two terms were over, I had already started looking around for something new.

While I took on a new role in a primary school with a British Curriculum in Jebel Ali on the other side of Dubai, Charlie found a job with HSBC in Dubai. Things were on the up at last and we traded in our tiny apartment for a small villa in Dubai itself. This time boasting two bedrooms, a garden and servants' quarters, it looked, finally, as though we were on our way to living the life of the expats we had heard about. It soon became clear however, that as much as I loved my new role, it was leading nowhere and so, after three happy years, I left the teaching profession and accepted a new role organising networking parties for the British Embassy.

While our professional lives were going in the right direction, rather than the move bringing Charlie and I together, as we had expected, our new roles were slowly driving us apart. Charlie was spending more time out of town with his job and I was increasingly seeking solace in our two new rescue dogs, Poppy and Winston. The pair soon became my focus for love and attention. The three of us would crawl under the fence of Mushraf Desert Park and find a quiet corner where we would go for long walks. Sitting on a sand dune, I would spend hours watching them race around, laughing at their antics and enjoy being alone with my thoughts under a vast darkening sky. We would often curl up on the sofa together giving each comfort and love. In the meantime, Charlie and I drifted apart.

Not wanting to give up on ten years of marriage, we went to counselling as a last resort. Perhaps we didn't really try hard enough. Eventually we decided to part and I finally had to accept that this person, who had been the other half of me for 13 years no longer featured in my future. It was heart wrenching. While Charlie stayed on in the villa with Poppy and Winston, I, once again, moved to a tiny, one-bedroom flat on the edge of town to start again.

For the first time since university I was facing life as a single girl but this time in a foreign country. Now that I was on my own again, I had to face the reality that I just couldn't survive on the meagre wages that my job with the British Embassy was bringing in. I was forced to move to something bigger and better and had to learn to manage my bank accounts and pay bills; something that, being married to a banker for ten years, I had managed to escape. Life was pretty basic and a far cry from the expat life I had been dreaming of, but learn I did. In fact, I frightened myself with my efficiency and had an uplifting sense of regaining my own identity.

I moved to an exhibitions and conference company where I was part of the team that put together Cityscape, a commercial property exhibition. This was an instant hit in the busy market of Dubai.

I had little money for the glittering parties however and since breaking up with my husband, chose to spurn the handsome men in their dinner jackets in favour of quiet nights of fun and games with our dogs, for whom I now shared custody. Several nights a week, I would pick them up and smuggle them into my flat, since dogs were not allowed. Not an easy feat when you consider that Winston was a Great Dane cross and Poppy only a little smaller. There were a few hilarious incidents when we would have to dash up the stairs instead of using the lift, but as Winston was terrified of climbing stairs it always ended with me staggering up three flights of stairs with 24 kilos of dog in my arms.

My apartment was in the middle of the desert in an area that was soon to be developed, but it did mean that their long runs were not sacrificed. We would often creep out at midnight and walk in the desert under the full moon. As the dogs tore around like lunatics, I would sit and drink in the stillness of the night, only to be rudely interrupted by one of them leaping on top of me for protection from the other as their games of chase continued. I was at my happiest with the dogs; they would make me laugh out loud, give me unconditional love and lick the tears off my face when I was sad.

Despite the success with the exhibition, it was time to move on and find a job that let me enjoy the high life.

Chapter One

All that glitters

Emma

This is the life, or is it?

'All that is gold does not glitter; not all those that wander are lost,'
JRR Tolkein

"More Champagne Madam?"

This was the life. This is why I had come to Dubai. Glittering parties, sparkling dresses, handsome men in their dinner jackets, uniformed waiters wearing spotless white gloves delivering an endless supply of champagne in sparkling crystal. Hmm...

I don't think so.

I had just spent five months in my second job since leaving the British Embassy, this time as director of sales and marketing for the Dubai office of a UK-based company. My role was to set up and launch a branch of the company that marketed a range of luxury goods, including cars and jewellery. This meant that I had to meet and mingle with many of the 'top' people in Dubai; the chief executives, the Sheikhs, dignitaries and decision makers.

The party invitations flowed as freely as the champagne. Finally I was beginning to sample the other side of life in Dubai. There were parties at Dubai's seven star hotel, The Burj Al Arab; launches of new companies and brands, with British royalty and a handful of local celebrities present too. There were luxury cars as giveaways and guests wearing bespoke jewellery to die for. It was a far cry from the life of a teacher that I had experienced when I arrived.

It was fantastic to start with, don't get me wrong, but after a while, the shiny veneer became increasingly tarnished. When I looked closely at what lay beneath, it could be shallow, boring and in some cases, plain unpleasant. In fact, after ten years it had become more and more difficult to hide my complete disinterest in the high life after all - and the people living it.

All the same, I was enjoying a lifestyle that I would not be able to afford in the UK; manicures, pedicures, waxing, hair appointments, coffee and my ironing done for me - all had become part of my normal everyday life and I felt that I was changing into a person that I didn't recognise. I was torn. Was I the same person that had once dreamt of owning dogs, horses and an open log fire to sit by? Was this new life the life I really wanted?

Jim

Reality check

'Ours is a world where people don't know what they want and they are willing to go through hell to get it.'
Don marquis

"Nice one, Jim," said Paul as my ball rolled with a gentle plop into the eighteenth hole. "Not enough to win the game, the Guinness is on you back at the Club House."

"Whatever you say, Boss." I replied shaking his hand through gritted teeth. I hated losing at golf and never let the boss win if I could help it.

We were on the smooth green turf of the Nad Al Sheba golf course and I had been in Dubai for almost three years.

This was no ordinary golf course; not only did it offer floodlit golf until midnight it also played host to the world's richest horserace - the Dubai World Cup. Big occasions like these teased me with buffets that confirmed the world really was my oyster, lobster and king-sized prawn. Shared hangovers and topping up the next day was the currency of expatriates and one I was happy to trade with. And yet for some reason, here I was, using the club as my solace for feeling lonely and empty.

My life in Dubai just wasn't sitting right. Whenever I pressed the pause button and allowed myself a scrap of quiet time it felt uncomfortable. I experienced immense feelings of isolation, guilt and greed like never before. My day-to-day life saw me sitting behind a lap top, locked up in a head office all day. Was this justification for my so-called 'higher' education? Not only had the marketing spend and sales results increased during my tenure but so had my waistline and blood pressure. I'd shot up from 90 to almost 100 kilos and my waist had gone from 34 to 38 inches. I had suddenly become known as 'Big Jim', but for all the wrong reasons.

I was fed up of using the last notch on my belt and despite the hairdryer of heat that hit me every time I got out of the 4x4 after work, returning to my flat to change before jumping into my roof-top pool still made it hard to feel refreshed. The combination of sauna, cold shower and pool even stopped doing the trick as I failed to settle after work and relax to enjoy my privileged surroundings, maintained so carefully by the faceless Indian workers that I had begun to call by name.

"Good morning Meester Jim," they would beam as I flopped into my pool before or after a hard day of emailing.

Sometimes I'd manage a grunt, and to go as far as looking them in the eye. As we began to exchange smiles, it got me thinking. Where did these guys come from, when did they have holidays? What did they eat? What did they earn? Their meagre reality provided me with some form of a benchmark whilst I was busy pitying my privileged existence. How did they feel being barely paid, largely ignored and probably taken for granted? What about the guy who filled my jeep with petrol? The pool cleaner? The countless subservient security guards who referred to me as 'Sir'? What had I done to deserve this accolade from a stranger?

These were the much ignored foot soldiers of Dubai who made the place work as they crouched down in their overalls in the midday sun or greeted everyone with a smile inside the air-conditioned restaurants. Thanks to all the so called self-help books I read by gurus like Phil McGraw, Tom Peters and Deepak Chopra I now realise that all that was happening was a bout of introspection. They call it 'self-discovery' but at the time it felt like downright misery. I was sick and tired of returning 'home' to my bachelor flat after another hard day of typing and shouting a sarcastic 'Hi, honey I'm home,' or a 'Home honey, I'm high,' out to the imaginary life partner who was waiting for me at the dining room table with a hug, a glass of red wine and a homemade lasagne.

GO! Read
The money or your life, John Clarke
Siddartha, Herman Hesse
Reimagine, Tom Peters

Occasionally, I'd return to the flat, polish off a bottle of wine and put my sorry self to bed. I stopped watching over-rated TV programmes opting instead to read more. I replayed films like Gladiator, empathising with Maximus as he is ordered to unveil himself. Had this been me in the twenty-first century, caught in my moment of glory, the scene might have gone something like this:

"My name is James William Wheat, commander of the Marketing Department, general of construction chemicals, loyal servant to the true emperor, my computer keyboard."

GO! Think:
Learn to enjoy your own company. If you cannot stand spending time with yourself, how can you expect anyone else to want to be around you?

When did you last allow yourself some quiet time?

So there I was, with everything that I thought I'd wanted and yet was still deeply unhappy. I had my health and material possessions. I was able to throw myself at the wondrous Dubai lifestyle while managing to stash some tax-free cash away from time to time. Mum always called this my Rainy Day Fund and maybe I was missing the rain after all. This spare cash only added to my feelings of selfishness, guilt, greed and isolation. Welcome to 'success'. What was my problem?

"Can you call a lady called Emma from this exhibition company, Jim?' Paul asked me one day in March. "I expect she'll be after some form of sponsorship."

"Yeah, yeah. Bring it on. You don't expect me to fall for that old ploy do you? They send in the blonde and I sign on the dotted line!"

I called her. She came into the office, bringing with her an air of such grace and femininity that it was as if the room were suddenly filled with flowers. Sitting on the opposite side of my huge desk, Emma began to describe the event she was planning for the upper echelons of the construction industry.

Emma, whom I discovered came from Devon, needed sponsorship. She was gorgeous. I signed.

Emma

'We all have big changes in our lives that are more or less a second chance'
Harrison Ford

Jim and I had a soft launch to our relationship.

We played some golf, he showed off his cooking skills and we took a trip out into the desert, all of which were male domains and designed to impress – and I was impressed. But I was then faced with having to do something in return – something that would have an impact on a man of such sporting prowess as Jim.

My opportunity arrived by chance about a week later, when I had some spare tickets to a work-related event: beach polo. It was glitzy and glamorous yet sporty, with a few stars thrown in for good measure and a boozy corporate lunch by the sea. It was a rather stark contrast to the testosterone-riddled rugby pitches and the ensuing pints of beer Jim was used to. My event had the requisite manly deeds and alcohol, but its handling was more refined. I even convinced myself he was just a potential client too. I was in heaven that day. Sunshine, glamour, horses and a handsome man whose full attention, somehow, I commanded all afternoon.

I found myself spending most of the afternoon gazing in Jim's direction. Once I realised that my attention was taken away from the horses and the men in white jodhpurs (which are two of my passions in life) I realised that Jim was not one to let go of in a hurry. If anything could drag my attention away from thighs and thoroughbreds, it had to be important. This realisation was enough to make me start looking at things a little differently.

GO! Think:
When something can't help but command your focus, it may be time to pay attention.

What commands your focus?

Thankfully, my attempts at trying to impress Jim had worked and that evening he called me to set an 'official' date for Valentine's Day. What better day to go public with our relationship?

Jim

One Gin & Tonic before Emma arrived wouldn't hurt, helped down with a handful of cashew nuts. It's the first date and she was bound to be a few minutes late. It would give me some company while I waited at the bar.

Emma

To add more romance to the evening, we had agreed to meet in the bar like semi strangers before going up to the restaurant. In my mind I had been playing the scene like an old black and white movie, with me as Audrey Hepburn standing in the doorway ... romantic music playing ... she is looking around uncertainly for the man of her dreams. their eyes lock ... she walks through a crowded bar ... all the men in the bar stop to follow her across the room until she locks into a passionate embrace with her man ... climax of music and cut.

In reality, the traffic was gridlocked and my phone was out of battery. The question was would he wait for me?

Jim

Having stared aimlessly into my second Tanquerey and tonic I began to wonder if she was going to show. Half an hour late was beyond first date late. Bloody Valentine's day. Nice cashew nuts.

Emma

Forty minutes later, (which I am not sure counts as 'fashionably' late) I was overjoyed to see Jim sitting patiently in a seat by the bar, looking gorgeous in a red shirt. I was so relieved that he had not given up and left, that the dignified film star entrance was forgotten as I rather unceremoniously flung myself into his arms bemoaning the traffic.

Jim

It was definitely worth the wait.

I had waited my whole life to experience the evening that we shared.

Emma

It was a wonderful evening on which to start our relationship. Now that we had admitted to ourselves and anyone who was interested - and many who weren't - that we were officially a couple, our relationship started to develop very quickly and we soon became constant companions.

Jim accompanied me devotedly to my work functions, each one became bigger and better than the last. The extravagance of it all made my head spin and my stomach churn. With Jim at my side, it was as if we began to share the same pair of eyes and together, as the rose-tinted lenses fell away, we both began to see the shallowness of Dubai society.

Jim

Clarity with Charity

'Charity: A thing that begins away from home, and usually stays there.'
    - Elbert Hubbard

Emma and I found it perfectly natural to share our thoughts, experiences and dreams as we compared corporate notes that were in essence very similar. I talked about how 'one day' I would resign to travel and write a book. This gave us a sense of perspective, it made our toils more worthwhile and whilst I was fantasising, Emma was dreaming of re-visiting South Africa and the South of France having spent memorable holidays where she had adored the simplicity and general way of life.

Another effective way I found that helped me to keep a sense of perspective was my obsession with physically pushing myself. The only exercise I took at work was walking up the stairs to my office, the odd pit stop for liquids in and out, and back down the stairs to leave again. It was hardly climbing Mount Everest although I did feel like I was hanging onto the corporate mountainside waiting for my pay cheque to land at the end of every month. I set myself sponsored challenges to do in my spare time to raise money for various local charities whilst keeping fit and keeping my feelings of guilt for my own ill-gotten wealth at bay. I'd already started planning more travel for that year and was pencilled in to do a charity trek with my friends at the Dubai-based charity, Gulf 4 Good, to discover the Machu Picchu site in Peru.

Thanks to the various charity challenges I had already cycled from Bangkok to Cambodia, climbed Mount Kilimanjaro and seen the wonders of the Serengeti. I know for a fact that the participants got as much out of it as the recipients of our donations. The more Gulf 4 Good trips I completed, the more I questioned why I was spending so much of my time in the office like a caged lion. Field sales had been my Serengeti and I was missing the real world Savannah.

These travel outlets were a brilliant way to get me out of the Dubai bubble. They kept me occupied and allowed me to spend less time in my empty, lonely, soulless flat. It may have been a trendy apartment for wannabes, with all mod-cons, minimalist furniture and a designer loo-roll holder, but before Emma I did not even have the luxury of a mouse or cockroach for company. So much for the 'high life'.

The final nail in the 'woe is me' coffin came when I flew to Sri Lanka in March 2005 to fly the corporate flag during some Tsunami relief work with the Japanese arm of the charity, Save the Children. I'd overheard in the office that my colleague, Graham, was due to visit the area on behalf of our Japanese operation to ensure that the $300,000 raised by the company through various fundraising initiatives was being put to proper use. I managed to convince the company to allow me to go with him to document our unsung work there after the devastation that had hit the island three months earlier.

GO! Think

Have you ever considered charity work? What local charity would you donate your time to? Do you think the charity really benefits or does it get swallowed up in administration?

I met Graham in the Hilton in Colombo, and we wasted no time in driving 100 miles along the south-east coast to the floodplains of Matara that were to benefit from some of the money. As we passed along the once idyllic coastline looking out at the seemingly calm ocean, we witnessed the scenes of destruction with open-mouthed disbelief. Whole communities, not just houses, had been pulled up from the roots of their foundations leaving nothing but destruction. The picture of the mangled wreckage of an eight-carriage commuter train will be with me forever.

Full of life until the wave struck and now skewed over the battered track it was hard to get my head around the enormity of what had happened; Imagine travelling on a train, reading one minute, only to be wiped clean out the next. The community had decided to leave the wreckage as it was, to honour the thousand people who had been annihilated as the tsunami stopped the train in its tracks. All that remained were bouquets of flowers, scribbled notes and the beginnings of rust.

What I had seen got me to thinking: I was full of life now, but for how long? When was my tidal wave going to hit?

Coming face to face with the locals, we met some very humble people who had lost not only all of their possessions but their family members too in - one fell swoop. They needed a leg-up to rebuild their lives. Our company had donated 25 concrete-block making machines together with 500 sewing machines, which left us with no doubt that our donation would at least make a small difference. We hoped to give these people the chance of earning a living again.

GO! Think
Why wait for the tidal wave to land? What changes can you make now in your life?

Back to my reality

'My problem lies in reconciling my gross habits with my net income.'
-Errol Flynn

On the business class flight home later that day I felt acutely uneasy. It just didn't seem right that the cost of my flight alone could have watered, fed and clothed a dozen of the families I had just seen for many months. Despite my feelings I soon succumbed once again to the lure of my privileged lifestyle and rather than stay and do something about the devastation I had seen, I boarded the plane.

That evening contrasted starkly with what I'd just witnessed as I accompanied Emma to a glitzy ball at one of Dubai's over the top 5 star hotels. In a matter of hours I had ricocheted from one guilt trip to another. The 250 or so exclusive guests all sipped champagne before sitting down to be entertained with a six-course meal and a couple of accomplished waiters-cum-opera singers. My fake smile was at its best as I failed to erase the scenes in Sri Lanka from my mind. Another glass of champagne seemed to help placate me and suitably numbed the memory of what I had just left behind. This was life with all its variety and I convinced myself that I was a lucky guy to have been able to experience such contrasts in the same day.

After this experience I found myself in more turmoil than ever. Every time I found myself settling back into Dubai-life and its luxury I would shake myself firmly.

The next day I started to wonder what mark I could make on the world, thinking perhaps irrationally that were I to die, then all the people I now knew would only bother to pay their last respects because of the eat-all-you-can curry on offer at the post-burial buffet. I didn't want it to be this way. I found myself awake in the early hours of the morning writing my epitaph as they suggest in self-help books, of which I was becoming so fond.

Two phrases stuck in my head during those long nights: 'A long time dead' and 'Seize the day'. I tried my best to start living by these idioms but for some reason there was still a void.

I'd had enough. There was nothing else for it. Sod waiting. Right here, right now was the only time. My stomach turned at the thought of waiting for however many years to pass as my sales charts were either applauded or booed. I wanted to get out of corporate life *and* Dubai. I wanted to discover myself; the real me.

GO! Think:
What would you like to be written on your headstone?

GO! Read:
Who will cry when you die? Robin Sharma

Emma

'We come to beginnings only at the end.'
   William Bridges

Jim resigned on April Fool's Day but not one person thought he was joking. On hearing the news, Jim's boss, Paul, offered his full support to his decision, and left him to create his own corporate Tsunami as he began setting his affairs in order, ready to hand over to his successor in three months' time.

On the evening of his resignation, we went up to the roof of my apartment and sat by the pool. We opened a bottle of vintage Shiraz that I had been saving to celebrate. He reassured me, however that this didn't mean the end of the relationship; just a few months apart.

"I feel like I have won the lottery. My feeling of excitement is unbelievable," he tried to explain as he wiggled the cork from the stronghold of the bottle.

"Aren't you just a little nervous, not having any concrete plans?" I coaxed gently. In his position, I'd have felt sick, not excited!

"Not at all. With no ties or responsibilities, anything is possible from here onwards. The only downside is the summer apart," he said looking at me for a reaction.

But I was determined to be positive. This was something he really wanted to do and I would only give him support, regardless of the fact that I was already dreading losing him.

To make it more bearable, we decided to take a holiday to South Africa at the beginning of July, after Jim had served his notice, then he would set off via the UK as a first step. Come October, we would be reunited. It didn't sound that bad. But in my heart, it didn't feel so good.

In truth, aside from the prospect of being without Jim for three months, his decision had really made me reflect on my own situation. With little support from the London office, I was becoming increasingly disillusioned with my job too, which had now grown to encompass being general manager and receptionist since the people in those roles had left. I was fed up; not just with the job, but with the constant round of parties, the small talk and the shallowness of the city. I felt that my values were being stepped on from a great height and I just didn't want to compromise any more.

Go! Think

What are *your* values?

How can you live in a way that is true to your values?

Just like Jim, I too wanted to do something that counted and sipping champagne just didn't cut it anymore. Something was missing.

Decision Time. Should I resign and take time out and go with Jim, or stay in Dubai and wait for his return?

Out came the corkscrew again and another bottle of my favourite red wine that I had been saving for another deserving occasion. It really needed a log fire for it to be fully appreciated, but an evening trying to decide whether my dreams were within my reach and budget seemed an appropriate time for this fine bottle.

But I now had financial commitments in property that I couldn't (and didn't want to) walk away from. And it wasn't just the money, either. I had been in Dubai for a long time and enjoyed most of it, looking on the emirate as my home. I had great friends there and wasn't sure that I wanted to give all that up.

Go! Read

Change your life in 7 days, Paul McKenna

After some thought and figure-juggling, I realised that if I was going to go, the only way I could make it work was by taking some unpaid leave, which meant selling my car. I was the very proud owner of a brand new Rav 4 that I had been driving for 18 months. I loved my car and the thought of parting with it was not pleasant. However, it meant that money would not be a worry if I took some time out. With the financial-problem solved, Jim and I raised a toast to our combined wisdom before knuckling down to the next dilemma – whether I should take a sabbatical or leave my job permanently.

With blue, slightly hazy skies, the morning of 25ᵗʰ April dawned just like any other in Dubai. The temperature was slowly starting to climb up the mercury scale and would reach 95°F by noon. Climbing into my car, which already felt like an oven, I wished as I often did at this time of year, that it was a convertible and set out for the office not thinking that this day would be any different from any other day at work. I fought my way through the congestion of cars that had already built up and crawled their way along the Sheikh Zayed Road. I took the time to really look around me. Glass-clad buildings of all shapes and sizes had sprung up from nowhere, hoardings with the promise of yet more new developments had been constructed and it seemed as if the Dubai dream had been plastered onto the 10-metre high boards and cranes as skyscrapers shaped the skyline for as far as the eye could see.

During my autopilot drives to work in the mornings, the extent of all of this had gone unnoticed; I remember looking at people as they too, drove to work, on that day. All the other drivers looked worried, half asleep or angry. It struck me that no-one looked happy or pleased to be driving to work at all.

On reaching the office, compelled by some unknown force, the first thing I did was go to my diary and count how many weeks remained until we left for our planned holiday to South Africa. Just over eight. That got me thinking. I counted again, this time to the end of the holiday. This time it was exactly three months. Three months including my full holiday entitlement – my official notice period. If I resigned there and then, I could give my notice and not be tied to coming back to Dubai after South Africa. It was all now possible.

One brief email to London later and I had resigned. And I hadn't even consulted Jim first. I was bursting to ring him with the news.

It was ironic, as on paper I had a wonderful job, was financially independent, owned a couple of properties, had a nice car, a great social life, could afford exotic holidays and had a fantastic man in my life. But materialism did not seem important anymore; I wanted to explore life, find my own 'joie de vivre'.

It seemed to me that all things had been conspiring against me, in a good way, to guide me into giving my resignation and now, it was all about to change. My hard-won and long-dreamed-of security was about to go out of the window of the vast second floor office where I had worked for the past five months. And I was overwhelmed with excitement, not feeling sick in the slightest.

GO! Think
What is your 'Joie de vivre'?

Calling Jim, I kept my fingers crossed he was not in a meeting ... He answered his mobile straight away.

"How would you like a travelling partner?" I asked.

Silence ensued, followed by an explosion of delight and a hundred and one questions. To say he was thrilled would not come close, but the decision was made, we would be travelling together and neither of us could contain our glee.

Jim

Leap of faith

'When one jumps over the edge, one is bound to land somewhere.'
   - D.H Lawrence

It was like taking that first step over the edge when you abseil; you know that you have ropes, harnesses and a helmet protecting you, but that first leap over the edge is terrifying until you feel the ropes take up the slack and you are held safely. We were stepping outside of our comfort zone. For the first time in many years, we had no plan for our long-term future. The stress of our jobs had been replaced by a bubbling excitement mixed with a flutter of butterflies in the pit of our stomachs every time the thought of what we were about to do flashed into our minds.

Emma and I spent the next few weeks making plans, re-making plans and then starting again from scratch. Jungle trips to the Amazon, cycling round France, a woodcutter's log cabin in South Africa. We listed our top 5 places we'd like to visit together.

GO! Think:
Where are the top five places you would like to visit?
Why?

We calculated how much money we could raise between us, what we needed to sell to make up the shortfall and reckoned we could travel for up to six months without getting into any serious debt. Although I'd been in a position of having the luxury of an additional *per diem* budget to spend I was now about to be spending my own cash whilst not earning a penny. It was time to opt out of the company pension and bring on the Rainy Day Fund!

Neither of us could say what we'd be doing nor where we would end up after our travels. But that was how we wanted it.

Less appetising however was the thought of updating our inoculations. A self-confessed needle-phobe, the experience left me tucked up in bed feeling sorry for myself whilst Emma took the needles in her stride. It was spiders that turned her into a quivering wreck. With insects galore highly likely on our trip, Emma gritted her teeth looking for a solution - and found one in an unexpected place.

Emma

Angels and arachnophobia
'You have brains in your head
You have feet in your shoes
You can steer yourself
Any direction you choose
You're on your own. And you know what you know
And YOU are the one who'll decide where to go,'
Dr. Seuss

Now that I had resigned and organised my possessions, my intense phobia of spiders was a major hurdle, and with Peru and the Amazon on the agenda, one I had to deal with. Fast.

My paranoia with spiders had reached ridiculous heights. To my mind, the fact that every spider has eight eyes in addition to eight legs is enough to instil fear into the most stoic of people. Spiders within a 10 metre radius of me used to pop out and show themselves just to see my reaction (yes, I did actually hear one laugh sadistically). I could never step on a spider to kill it as I had learned years earlier that they never die, they just crawl up through the sole of your shoe, up your leg and wait for their chance to make their presence known.

Finally, I could not walk past one as it is another well-known fact that spiders jump on you when you are not looking, then crawl up your back and into your hair. If any of the above happened (or even nearly happened), I would go into hysterics, shouting, screaming and crying, real tears of fear.

The solution came in the form of hypnotherapy. Laura, a good friend of Jim's, was not only a qualified hypnotherapist but also did Ka-huna massage, a holistic approach to healing, which balances the body and mind in all its physical, emotional and spiritual elements. She suggested that I try a few sessions to see what happened.

By the end, I pictured these very frightening creatures wearing red wellies on each of their eight legs, looking utterly ridiculous. That would certainly wipe the grin off their faces the next time they popped out to say hello. The red wellies really helped and though I still did not like the thought of them being in close proximity to me, at least the irrational fear seemed to have gone. My body, mind and soul were prepared to face anything that came my way. But I guessed I would have to wait until the Amazon to really put it to the test.

Having made such a scary yet exciting decision and quit my job, I also wanted reassurance that I was making the right choice and that my future looked fantastic. Not much to ask really. Part of Laura's sessions gave you the choice to pick out some cards that were 'messages from your angels'. Angel Cards are a kind of Tarot and are supposed to sum up the current situation and I was eager to see what message they had for me.

The three cards that I pulled out of a pack were:

All is well: 'Everything is happening exactly as it's supposed to, with hidden blessings you will soon understand.'

You Know What to Do: 'Trust your inner knowledge, and act upon it without delay.'

Spread Your Wings: 'Don't hold back right now. The timing is perfect, and you're ready to soar.'

Pretty powerful messages and it was good to get a second opinion, despite what my instinct said. One final card left me in no doubt that I was doing the right thing. Not long before, my beloved dog Winston had been poisoned whilst walking in the desert and died within ten minutes. Nothing could have been done to save him. I was devastated and after the experience, I was not looking forward to leaving Poppy behind, even though she was greatly loved and cared for by my ex-husband Charlie. The card I pulled took even Laura aback as she had not come across it before:

Pets: 'Your pets, whether in Heaven or on Earth are happy

and being looked after by the Angels.'

Well I couldn't have asked for any more reassurance. A few days later, I received a call from Charlie, who had remarried six months earlier, saying that he was emigrating to New Zealand with his new wife and would be taking Poppy with him. Although I was initially devastated that I wouldn't see her again, I had to smile at the thought of her running around the green hills having the freedom that dogs do not have in Dubai. They would all be leaving within a day or two of us going off on our six months of travel, so all was well.

GO! Think:
Reassurance is great, but think about what *you* really want. Do you need someone else's permission to go after your dreams?

Jim

'There are times when silence has the loudest voice.'
Leroy Bronlow

Things were taking shape but despite my new Bohemian tendencies, I still had a niggling worry about hanging onto my Dubai flat whilst I was away. The rent on the flat alone would cost a third of the money we needed for the whole trip and rates across the city were busy increasing twofold in some cases. Miraculously, my company agreed to take over my flat while we were away agreeing to allow me to lock away our chattels in the spare bedroom.

"It's all working out for us," remarked Emma as she stuffed yet another pair of shoes into the chest of drawers. "It's the Angels."

"We'll need their help if you're going to buy any more shoes," I tutted, holding up a pair of pointless strappy sandals. Having cancelled my pension, cashed in my Rainy Day Fund and topped up my Karma points by investing in a few sessions with Laura myself, I felt ready to sell my collection of 150 once-watched DVDs before putting in my last day at work at the end of June. My last day arrived and I was called into the head honcho's office, regional president (and Paul's boss) Dick, for an exit interview.

"So, you're leaving us to go and exist on a higher plain then, Jim?" Dick asked wryly as he showed me to one of the swanky black leather executive chairs in his large sparse corner office. "Tell me, how would you run this company if you were in my shoes?" he said, staring at me intently whilst tapping the desk with the end of his pen.

This was my chance, but I was dumbfounded. For once in my life I really didn't know what to say and ended up sitting there mumbling 'one thousand two thousand three thousand four thousand,' hoping Dick would answer for me. All my hard won in-depth strategic knowledge and organisational skills had sunk to my boots. I'd reached 12 thousand when I was finally put out of my misery.

"Look. I'll give you a minute to think about it. I'm popping out for a moment."

Right I thought, now's my chance to tell him what I think of corporate hierarchy, those who pull their weight and those who don't and some of the great brainstorming sessions I would implement. This is the time to tell him how I would propose turning us into the best marketing department the world had ever seen. He returned in no time.

"Well then Jim, what would you do?"

Just as I was about to be shown the door I replied: "I'll tell you in six months when I've returned from my travels."

It was the best I could do and let go of the fact that it wasn't a question I had to answer.

Then silence. I bit my tongue and started counting from one thousand again. Say nothing Jimmy boy, nothing.

"Good answer. Do that, will you?" he replied as he led me

downstairs to tie up some formalities with the paperwork - or so I thought anyway. As we entered the conference room a good majority of the office and field-based staff were all sitting there with their backs to me. They all turned around as we walked in and started to cheer. I'd been well and truly set up and was delighted. It was a wise move keeping a measured tongue during my exit interview to avoid any egg on my face.

Dick gave a speech that was filled with praise.

GO! Read:
The art of war for executives by Sun Tzo

"Most of us would love to be in your shoes, Jim," he said. "But very few have the guts to do so and would leave the rat race if we had the courage."

I was dumbfounded.

"Safe travels. We wish you well and enjoy smelling the flowers," he concluded as the applause began.

I was presented not with a carriage clock but with a travel clock and silver compass. Both were engraved with good luck messages and the perfect gifts: pocket-sized and made for travel. Symbolically, they captured the fact that I wasn't sure where I was headed for, nor indeed even when I'd return. But I'd left a door open and that was the main thing.

GO! Think:
Where do you want to go with your life?

Emma

'None of us knows what the next change is going to be, what unexpected opportunity is just around the corner, waiting a few months or a few years to change all the tenor of our lives.'
Kathleen Norris

Our departure date was fast approaching and we said a fond farewell to our friends in the best way possible with a party.

Familiar faces and the laughter drowned out the background music as the volume of the babble of excited voices rose. We toasted the first leg of our trip with South African Pinotage and Chenin Blanc and beer flowed freely in true Dubai style.

Everyone came and none wanted to leave. We lingered st midnight, when the moon was high in a deep black, star-filled sky.

The next morning as we lay in bed listening to the song of the Mullah in the mosque, calling Muslims to prayer, amplified our hangovers. We realised how we had come to take that mystical sound completely for granted. This time we listened to every syllable even though we still, after a combined total of 15 years, did not understand a word he sang. We wondered if he ever saw the world's richest horse race, international tennis and golf tournaments or threw himself at a month-long shopping festival. Did he relish the thought of Burj Dubai, The World's tallest building becoming a reality that would look down on his mosque or was he praying that things could stay exactly the same?

GO! Think:
What conscious choices are you making in your life?

Can I pack my whole wardrobe?

Jim

'We only possess the things we put to use,'
  La Fontaine

It took us three more days to finish packing. Deciding what you really need for six months is no easy task, particularly when all you have is 25 kilos of luggage allowance per person. In the end we categorised our stuff into three piles:

'must have'

'nice to have'

'do you really need 15 handbags and twelve pairs of shoes, love?'

Emma

'If the shoe fits...buy two pairs'
Ralph Waldo Emerson

Why don't men understand that every occasion calls for its own pair of shoes? During the six months of travelling, I had to be prepared for an array of events, all of which called for their very own pair of shoes.

Go! Read
Why men don't have a clue and women always need more shoes, Barbara and Allan Pease

Jim

One black pair, one brown pair, trainers, sandals, slippers fair enough. All the others were surplus to any requirements, particularly as we were travelling. Emma's case was beginning to look like a second hand shoe fest.

Emma

A summer wedding (strappy sandals), summer in the UK (this could involve my whole wardrobe as the weather is so unpredictable), trekking (walking shoes), horse riding (riding boots), golf (golf shoes), at least one smart party (different pair of strappy sandals), possible Christmas balls (evening shoes), a beach holiday (flip-flops), a holiday with my mother (involves dressing for dinner so more smart shoes needed) and shoes for any other eventuality that may have cropped up.

Jim

The excuse was 'because the shoes had to match the handbags', or the clothes at least, which was another major girlie packing issue. I had to remind Emma that there would be water and soap so that we would be able to have clean clothes most of the time.

Emma

Then of course, the clothes had to match. It was one thing to have been able to get everything in our suitcases, which we were going to use as a base, but how on earth was I going to manage to squeeze my clothes and shoes into one (to me) tiny rucksack for our two-month ramble around Peru that we had planned? Perhaps they would have invented a *Harry Potter* type bag by then? You know the sort; the one that you can pack your entire wardrobe in, only weigh five kilos and is the size of a beach bag? I had my fingers crossed that they would have invented one by July.

Jim

Even sitting on her overloaded suitcases didn't do the trick. There was no way we'd fit all the junk she'd packed. We locked away our 'nice to haves' in the spare room of my flat and headed out like a magician and his assistant weighed down with their props. It would need more than a magic trick to make sure all our stuff would stay with us and survive our travels.

Go! Read
Free Agent Nation, Daniel Pink

Emma

The answer to our prayers came in the shape of shipping some of our things back to the UK via DHL. Packing our 'mega' boxes which were bound for England while we travelled to South Africa was probably the hardest part of all the logistics of our travels. The items that we packed in our respective boxes went something like this:

His:
- Gortex Jacket for hiking
- Ski gloves (were we really expecting snow?)
- Three pairs of trainers (and he thinks *I'm* extravagant with shoes)
- Books to read (plenty, because, of course, they may not be available in the UK)
- Five or six day-pack rucksacks (it's important to coordinate with your anorak)
- Compasses (plural - because 'you have to have a back up')
- Water carriers for the rucksacks (also known as camel-packs, in case we trek across the Sahara)
- Leather coat he has never worn ('but it smells good')
- Another pair of trainers ('just in case')

Hers:
- Shoes (a few pairs)
- Handbags (two)
- Shoes (a few more pairs I forgot about, to cover all eventualities)
- One large handbag (to double as an overnight bag)
- A couple of books
- Lime green leather jacket (no warmth value, but it looks good)
- One more pair of shoes (I may need these for the wedding in Scotland)
- A fake fur hat for our Christmas jaunt to church.

After teasing each other about our travel items, it became clear that we had very different ideas about essentials, so, we left each other in peace, to pack uninterrupted. Neither of us had quite mastered the art of travelling light, but in my defence, I was packing for the unknown (and potentially all eventualities: a summer and winter in England, a wedding in Scotland, and one in Dubai, trekking in Peru and a stop off in France) and figured it would be cheaper to take things with me than buy them new if I suddenly needed them.

GO Think!

Respect what other people value; while we were packing, both of us had our own reasons for wanting to take a particular item with us. Individuality was the mutual attraction. Try not to change what they do or how they think. Just accept it.

Jim

Weight on my mind

Admittedly the DHL mega boxes came in handy. I just about managed to strain the locks shut on my battered Delsey case, and my 80-litre Karrimor (if only it could) rucksack.

Emma

After all of Jim's nagging over what I was packing, he soon stopped when the lady at check in charged him excess baggage. Looking in disbelief that his luggage could possibly weigh more than mine, which contained the second hand shoe shop, he managed to justify the whole situation.

"Well, I am much taller than you, so my clothes take up much more space and therefore weigh more– what do you expect?" he grinned.

Our travels had begun First stop: South Africa. What lay

ahead only time would tell.

Go! Do It:

1. Write down a list of 5 important things you want in your life.

   Have the courage not to lose sight of what you want or what makes you happy. Do not be blinded by distractions on your journey to get there. Other people may have different opinions, but it is you that counts.

2. Write down what you would have to say no to, in order to make sure they are in your life. What would you be saying yes to?

   The list of no's are the things you will no longer let get in the way of what you want in your life.

Chapter Two

Wine and Braai

Jim

Goodbye Dubai

'No man is an island, entire of itself; every man is a piece of the continent.'
John Donne

Having grudgingly settled up my excess baggage charge at Dubai's clinically clean airport I treated myself to a coffee. Before I was halfway down my steaming cinnamon topped skinny latte, I proceeded to bend Emma's ear about Dubai, wondering what the place had in store for us when we returned from our travels. My obsessive 'what ifs?' were interrupted by Emma:

"This is Day One, Jim, and I'm hoping that there will be many more ahead of us. Can we just go with the flow and see what opportunities present themselves as we travel?" she queried, scooping a teaspoon of fluffy froth from the top of her latte.

"Oh come on," I groaned, "can't you just hypothesise for a moment and fast forward six months right here, right now? I'd like to weigh up what our options might be before we get on the plane." I knew my plea was pointless even before I'd finished saying it.

"No way, Mr Caffeine," Emma said quickly, sliding her hand over the formica-topped table to make a grab for my paper cup. "You're being a complete handful. I'm going to make this the last one you're having for a lo-o-ong time."

"I'm only having half a cup," I whined. "Like it makes a difference?"

"Oh but it does," she replied. "You're frothing at the mouth, your pupils are dilated and before we know it you'll be shaking. Let's leave the rest of the coffee shall we?' she demanded, reaching for my cup again.

I felt like the four-year old I once was who was having his E numbers whisked away from him. Rather than bang my head on the floor in protest I left my steaming potion and headed for the sleepy departure lounge. Our plane rose with the sun leaving an unusually peaceful Dubai behind. My caffeine enhanced mind raced and wondered what the next six months had in store for us.

As we gained altitude, I caught a glimpse of the once barren, mint-blue sea that was now smothered with those 'build and they will come' Palm Island and The World projects; two man-made archipelagos. I knew that these alone were set to just about treble Dubai's coastline from 45 to 120 miles ... I thought The Palm was pushing it in terms of feasibility but The World really took the biscuit. Peering down on the first scattering of what promised to become 280 man-made islands, shaped like the world, made me draw comparisons of how we were building our world from scratch form this day forth.

The Dubai I had known was fast becoming Vegas-On-Sea, where real men gambled with real money, but in real estate as casinos are banned in the United Arab Emirates. Watching our world as we had known it slip away, I could not get my mind off the craziness of the construction down below. I couldn't get my head around who was crazier: Dubai for its islands and someone actually showing an interest in buying one or us for quitting our jobs to travel for half a year with no income between us. From here on in we really were entering our own little world. First stop: South Africa.

GO! Read –
1,000 Places To Visit Before You Die, A traveller's Life list, Patricia Shultz.

Emma

First stop was a five star hotel. I looked forward to unwinding in a little luxury; I planned to make the most of every second as it would not be long before crisp white linen sheets were replaced by polyester sleeping bags, torrential rain and jungle fever.

Despite all its troubles I had always had a soft spot for South Africa. People always told me that the sky was bigger in Africa and until I saw it, I didn't understand what they meant. It was not only bigger, but it was a deep, unending blue that was never the same in any other country.

But that would be Cape Town. Jo'burg, as it is affectionately known, was different: great shops, but a rather frightening city, filled with violence, car-jackings and murders; a place where people walk their dogs with a baseball bat in their hand. Clusters of people stand at the traffic lights, trying to force leaflets through your car windows or to sell you stuff, simply adding to the nervousness of drivers. Even in broad daylight it is not uncommon for a leaflet to be swapped for a gun.

From start to finish, the experience was a roller coaster, which had me clinging to my seat for dear life. Being picked up in a Mercedes from the airport and taken to the hotel was probably one of the few times I had wished I were riding in a battered pick up truck. As the epitome of a wealthy, moving target for car-jackers, I spent the entire journey hoping that my Guardian Angel was on duty that morning.

On (thankfully safe) arrival at the hotel reception, we were greeted by what looked like a mountain of sunshine. An arrangement of yellow stargazer lilies in the middle of the lobby took my breath away. Not just because of its size – it was taller than I was and must easily have been just as wide too – but the scent that filled the air was as thick as butter. Dick had instructed us to 'smell the flowers', here on our first day; we had no choice.

"Come on Jim, be brave and take a step closer and smell them," I urged as we waited to check in.

"They look lovely but I am sure they smell like air freshener," he grumbled pulling back. "A flower is just a flower after all."

GO! Think
When was the last time you stopped to smell the flowers?

Jim
Treated royally

'First you take a drink, then the drink takes a drink, then the drink takes you.'
Francis Scott Key Fitzgerald

It was hard to believe that we were only 30 minutes from claustrophobic Jo'berg airport and a couple of thousand miles from furnace-hot Dubai. My mobile phone hadn't rung with requests from the office, colleagues or anybody else for that matter. This would take some getting used to, not even a text!

We sucked up every last drop of the obsessively landscaped hotel garden where we decided to have lunch that day: the flame-red hibiscus the size of oak trees, water features full of Koi carp and a wine waiter at our service. This setting immediate slowed down our perception of reality, like those endless days of the summer school holiday that just seemed to go on and on. Time stood still.

GO! THINK
When did time stand still for you last?

Back to our wine waiter, the spitting image of the Queen's middle son. 'Prince Andrew', who was really called Nicolas, hailed from the Winelands and his job enabled him to express his knowledge of and passion for grapes.

It's true to say that although I enjoy a glass of wine I don't know my Shiraz from my Chardonnay, nor my Blue Nun from my paint thinners. Our enthusiastic Prince however, kept wheeling out another glass for us to try with different foods and demonstrated how the taste and colour of wine changes depending on what you eat with it and how long it's in the glass. Zipping effortlessly between tables he pointed towards an ancient marble fountain that stood in the centre of a crossroads of gravelled walkways and before he could give us another grape fact I asked:

"Is it Chardonnay that comes out of the fountain Nicolas?" mentioning the only brand I knew how to pronounce.

"Hey, I wish, now there's an idea, imagine that!" replied our wide-eyed wine buff as he effortlessly opened another bottle of whatever it was.

"What about chocolate?" added Emma.

"Wine and chocolate *az-well*, now that would make for trouble, eh?" he chuckled.

Nicolas returned to *his* passion and launched into his top 10 vineyards to visit in the Cape. As the 'really must try' list came to an end a complimentary cheese platter that could have fed half of Soweto, was brought out to soak up our alcoholic excesses. It seemed impossible that our idyllic afternoon could have got any better when my slurring comrade announced that 'shopping was off' and it was best we retired to bed for a power nap. In mutual agreement we finished off with a dizzying 'must try' port before staggering back to our room. Our eyes were shut before the sun set as the power nap turned into a sleepathon.

We kidded ourselves that drinking a pint of water would prevent the hangover from hell in the morning. I think we needed a gallon. I suffered from practically no sleep due to dehydration, indigestion, heartburn and trapped wind. Sadly, I was no longer 18 years old and processing debauchery wasn't as easy as it used to be. From the morning's caffeine to the evening wines, I had learned my lesson and it was time I got a grip.

Sadly the next morning, shopping suddenly reappeared on the agenda. My head hurt. I looked like I'd slept with my head in a trouser press so I decided to leave Emma to her devices while I worked off the excesses in the hotel gym.

Emma

'We don't see things as they are, we see them as we are.'
   Anaïs Nin

While Jim huffed and puffed in the gym, my plans didn't need for him to be with me, so, after a leisurely breakfast morning, I took myself off to the mall.

Standing in the sunshine, waiting for the hotel car to arrive, I was approached by a very tall, liveried black man, with the broadest grin I had ever seen. His gold-embossed badge told me his name was Litre.

"Good morning, ma'am," he called out to me. "Would you like me to clean your shoes?"

Litre had a face filled with hope and happiness. Rather than catch my taxi, I felt compelled to find a shady swing seat beneath the lush greenery outside the hotel and sit and talk to him for hours. In reality I perched on a kind of stationary sedan chair above his cleaning equipment near the entrance to the hotel.

Being in full view of the guests like that, and involved in a role that was resonant of the Deep South of America and slavery, it felt very uncomfortable. But I really wanted to talk to Litre.

Jim

After I'd worked my chest and arms I was feeling dizzy, dehydration most probably.

Emma

He lived in the Soweto township in a 'shack house' that accommodated eight people, including his wife, two children, brothers and mother. I had seen these 'shack houses' on previous trips and knew they were little more than pieces of corrugated iron arranged to provide a rudimentary shelter. I could still picture the poverty and squalor I had seen on my last visit. Litre was proud of his job as it meant he could provide for his family; both of his children had the luxury of going to school, which was a privilege, not the norm in the townships. Above all, he enjoyed the contact he had with people every day. Litre's job would mean that his family would live in one of the better houses and would have food on the table.

He took the greatest pride in his work and I have to say that my high, black ankle boots looked amazing. To come face to face with someone who had so little yet who took such pride in his work and possessed such a cheerful outlook, struck a chord. Why should we be conditioned to pity people like him? In many ways he had achieved more than we had.

'All but death, can be adjusted
Dynasties repaired
Systems settled in their sockets
Citadels dissolved
Wasted of lives resown with colours
By succeeding springs
Death unto itself exception
Is exempt from change.'
Emily Dickinson

I sat in my taxi in my shiny boots but I felt unsettled. I felt uncomfortable at the mall too. I was getting worried. I wasn't in the mood for shopping despite the lure of new shops bearing items not yet available in Dubai. As I entered, the mall was starting to come to life. The big steel shutters were still being raised. I wandered around aimlessly unable to focus on anything.

Jim

I should have given my shoulder exercises a miss as part of last night's debauchery came back up, practically mid press.

Emma

An overwhelming feeling that I shouldn't be there kept nagging at me. As the morning progressed, the mall soon filled up with shoppers, all intent on their mission; all that is, except me. Not even finding a pack of the angel cards that Laura had recommended could lift my spirits. With an hour left before the car returned for me, I gave up hope of shopping and decided to go back up to the front of the mall and sit in the sunshine while I waited.

Have you ever made a split second decision that, in hindsight would have a major impact on your life?

I did that day.

Waiting for the lift back to the ground floor, I noticed a guy who was standing beside me. Obviously in a hurry, he was very agitated and kept pressing the call button as though his life depended on it. He was young, about mid thirties, black, with a kind face and smiling eyes, although that morning, clouded by a frown. He was smartly dressed, wearing some kind of security uniform. As the lift doors opened, he leapt in and looked at me to see if I was planning on following him.

"You go ahead," I heard myself saying as I decided not to join him in the lift after all.

"I don't want to be near you when you get shot," I thought silently.

Don't ask me where that came from. It was a fleeting thought that was gone before it really had time to develop. We were in the middle of a busy shopping mall in broad daylight. I had no logical reason to have thoughts like that. But the city's reputation was in the forefront of my mind.

Jim

Enough was enough, a shower and sauna then back to bed.

Emma

As I had irrationally declined the offer of a ride in the lift, I had to find the escalators; if I was suddenly to become fussy over all my lift companions, I could be there all day.

On reaching the top of the escalator, I heard a commotion with shouting followed by people running. As I took a couple of steps forward, I knew instinctively why I had felt unsettled that morning and why I had had strange thoughts about security guards being shot: there on the floor outside the bank where he worked, lying dead in a pool of his own blood, was the very same security guard.

Everything slowed down, like a scene from a movie, but life carried on. People were going about their business as the murdered security guard's colleagues tried to give him some dignity in death. Someone placed a jacket over his face, while another unravelled a large sheet of blue plastic that would later cover his body. The odd shopper took a detour to get a closer look, seemingly out of curiosity rather than genuine concern, but most of the people carried on walking past the body without even a second glance as though they were used to such events disrupting their shopping expeditions. When a plastic cordon was put across the mall, blocking people's routes, there was nearly an outcry. People were more concerned about not getting to their favourite shop than they were about a dead body, someone's son, maybe father, lying on the floor.

This was all observed in a matter of about a minute, but it seemed like I was rooted to the spot for much longer. The hurried footsteps of the police, with guns blazing, brought me back to reality.

Isn't it strange how life can change in a split second? He would have left his family that morning, making the promise to see them later that evening, not realising that it was his last goodbye. Realising I was shaking like a withdrawing alcoholic, tears pouring down my face, I started the fatal 'what if' scenarios:

Jim
Midday and still no sign of Emma no doubt maxing the credit card out.

Emma
- What if I had taken a ride in the lift instead of the escalator, would I have been there with him?
- What if the shooting had been a few seconds later as I was walking past him?
- What if they had missed him…?

At that point I stopped. My Guardian Angel had most certainly been on duty that morning and for that, I would be eternally grateful.

Go! Read
Spirit Guides and Angel Guardians, Richard Webster

But why was I so upset? Maybe, because of his family he had left behind that morning. Maybe because no-one seemed to be worried that there was a body on the floor or maybe it was just because life seemed so cheap. Whatever the reason, it seemed to have touched my soul deep down and I wanted to weep like a child for the life lost. I went outside and waited for the car to take me safely back to what I now felt was my very privileged world.

GO! Think
What do you say to your friends and family when you say goodbye? Do they know how you feel about them?

Jim

Flying therapy

'I fly because it releases my mind from the tyranny of petty things.'

John Donne

The flight to Cape Town soon diverted any lingering thoughts of our experiences of Jo'burg. I would like to say that it was the stunning scenery during the flight that took my mind off it, but our diversion happened before we had even left the ground. In planning this trip, I had taken the budget option on flights to Cape Town (you never know when the saving will equate to a pair of shoes), which I had been recommended by a friend who often visits the Cape.

On approaching the terminal there was a huge billboard advertising Kulula Airline reading 'Distant relatives, unfortunately closer now'.

Brilliant. Being from marketing backgrounds this kept us amused until we were on the plane and built up our anticipation of the in-flight announcements, which we had been told were as hilarious.

They were not wrong.

"In the event of ditching in water, would those who can swim please line up on the right hand of the plane and those who can't on the left," instructed a very serious tannoy voice.

More announcements like this followed throughout the flight eventually ending with:

"Please don't leave your belongings behind, especially your mother-in-law. We have been trying to get rid of ours for years, we don't want yours. We hope you have enjoyed flying with us as much as we have enjoyed taking you for a ride."

It was fantastic and Cape Town put on quite a show for our arrival with more brilliant sunshine, blue skies and a scattering of wispy cloud hovering around Table Mountain. I heaved a sigh of relief. This was the South Africa I had fallen in love with.

Jim

Judging a book

'Try the manners of different nations first-hand before forming an opinion about them.'
Robert Louis Stevenson

Our base for the following week was a self-catering set up called Rose Cottage, tucked under the formidable rock-faced apostles in Camps Bay. Our warm hosts, Pam and Steve, made us feel very welcome as did their two big daft Doberman dogs. We helped ourselves to their library of books and for the first time in years I read a book that made me feel as free as a bird and enjoyed every minute of it.

GO! Read
The Seagull Jonathan Livingston , Richard Bach

It wasn't all about the book club. With us in the shadows of the infamous Table Mountain, with its trademark cloth-like veil of mist that often covered the 1,000 metre summit, it was there to climb. Early next day we took a local reccy, meandering up towards the foot of the twelve apostles, soaking up the views, the fresh air and the birdsong.

We were snapped out of our ambling when a battered old white transit pulled up beside us. The driver resembled Mike Tyson and hid behind a pair of oversized mirrored sunglasses. Our hearts stopped beating for a moment.

"Do you know where the Shell garage is please?" he asked.

We tried our hardest not to look too much like tourists as I simultaneously seemed to develop more of a strut and a swagger than a walk in an attempt to seem like a local.

"Excuse me," he persisted, "do you know where the Shell garage is?" he asked again as he continued kerb crawling alongside us with his tyre-like arm leaning casually out of the driver's side door. Suddenly it felt like we were part of a re-enactment for some macabre crime.

"Yes," I trembled and gesticulated in the direction from which we had just come. "It's back down the hill, turn left at the end and it's right in front of you." Where was the nearest armed response team when I needed them? I held my breath and listened to my heart pounding as I waited for a gun to be pulled. My hand stuck clammily to Em's.

"OK, thanks and go well," he beamed giving us an appreciative thumbs up as he did a swift U turn and sped off in the opposite direction.

I allowed myself another tiny swagger and shrugged it off in front of Em but inside I felt ashamed for doubting him. After Emma's experience in Jo'Burg I was instinctively judgemental, leaning towards paranoid. I wondered whether I would have reacted the same if a white guy had pulled up in a spanking new black transit van? We had to be careful as all travellers do, but what was the balance between struggling to let down our guards too far and opening our arms to everyone that we met?

GO! Think

Try and maintain a balance of not pre judging a situation but being wary of what may happen at any given time.

There is a balance.

What is your balance?

Emma

Much to 'Mr. Sergeant Major's disappointment we ended up taking a cable car, although for one heart-stopping moment, Jim was adamant about climbing up the mountain instead.

"It will be a great introduction to training for Machu Picchu," he announced with conviction.

"I would prefer to stick to climbing the steps up to the cable car as my introduction to training after yesterday's performance," I reminded him gently.

You see, the previous evening's walk from Camp's Bay – a 20 minute 'stroll' had very quickly reminded us how unfit we had become. We had taken our stroll in silence, due simply to the fact that we were both so out of breath. I was certain that we were not quite ready to mount an attack on Table Mountain without the aid of a cable car. Sense prevailed and we enjoyed the sights from the top of the mountain like every other sensible tourist. Our training for Peru's Inca Trail could wait for another day.

The kaleidoscope of the Cape worked its magic on us both; glorious sunny days with a large topaz sky, majestic coastal scenery, cloaks of green velvet on the hills meeting endless stretches of white sandy beaches, richly flavoured and spiced local food, full bodied wines to tantalise the taste buds all mixed together with the occasional log fire and wonderful aroma of wood smoke. Cape Town is one of the most colourful cities that I have ever visited, not only in terms of the abundance of painted architecture, mostly in the Malay Quarter, but also the cultural diversity of the people who live side by side in a city whose biggest claim to fame used to be apartheid.

Street cafés add to the vibrancy of the waterfront, which crawls with tourists and performing artists, all enjoying the majestic backdrop of Table Mountain that watches over the city like a sleeping giant. The harbour's heady mix of diesel fumes and sea air give it that distinct maritime smell. After a few days in Cape Town I started to relax. Jim on the other hand was stressed that his phone had not rung, but was slowly beginning to ease into holiday mode.

Jim

Cape melée

'A whale is harpooned only when it spouts.'
Henry Hillman

Lunch at Simonstown's Black Marlin came highly recommended by 'Prince Andrew' of Jo'Burg although the waiter gave us the bad news that we were about a month too early whale wise but they did have a great lunch menu all the same. Whales were on my list of things to say I'd done. Emma remained frustratingly undecided between eating the tuna, yellowtail or marlin.

Meanwhile, a table of Americans strained with excitement as they made a flurry of calls on their mobile phones. They hadn't seen any whales either but heard that London had just been awarded the 2012 Olympics. And a series of bombs had gone off that morning, paralysing the capital. Emma and I quickly came back down to earth with a bump. One call to London later, the information we had was very sketchy but we counted our blessings once again and realised that few places were safe these days. Emma quickly chose the tuna.

A few minutes later the restaurant was rocked again, this time by the news that the Americans had spotted a vast whale in the sea and clamoured in turn for the only pair of binoculars in the establishment. We were delighted to get a turn too and soon enjoyed a close up of a rare humpback as we finished off our trout with herbed spinach. We raised a toast to London in-between the nonchalant blows of our first whale and appreciated what a surreal contrast we had just experienced. We'd both been on buses in London over the years and although there was an infinitely small chance of getting caught up in such an atrocity, the odds didn't make it any more acceptable. We learned many things that day, not least that the key to whale spotting is to listen out for the hollow blows of air or to look for the spout of sea water, not the splash of the fin as we'd first thought.

GO! Think
What gives you the feeling of contentment?

Emma

'Beyond mountains there are mountains again.'
   Haitian Proverb

We left the tranquillity of Camp's Bay ready to take in the splendour of the Winelands. This time we were staying in more basic accommodation. it was to break us into what lay ahead over the next few months. My cunning plan was to start in five-star splendour and slowly acclimatise to the possibility of camping. The only obligatory criteria whilst planning the trip was that the accommodation had a log fire. We both loved sitting in front of the fire, but Jim was a fire pervert; if it could burn and wasn't nailed down it would end up in the flames. Pyromania kept him amused for hours. Jim is a cave man at heart who loves nothing more than fire gazing after a hard day's hunt.

I couldn't wait to get exploring around all the vineyards in the valley. But Jim had different thoughts. Ten days of wine excess had taken its toll. He had woken up feeling like a Boy Scout raring to take off into the hills with his map and compass. Was he crazy? We were in the Winelands for heaven's sake. That was like going to Blackpool and not seeing the lights or going on a ride. But no, he was adamant, enough wine, he needed exercise and from now on needed to earn his food.

That was all I needed.

Fortunately I came up with another cunning plan. I don't like to say 'compromise', because that always ends up with one of you not doing what you want, so the solution I thought of was one of those rare win-win situations. Bikes. We could hire mountain bikes and *cycle* around the vineyards, which would keep both of us smiling. This was our first mistake of the day. Little did I know that this was going to come back and bite me on the (very sore) bottom.

With the sun shining on our backs and the road gently sloping down towards where we were headed we couldn't have asked for anything more. Except for a map that was to scale, perhaps?

My map indicated that the town of Franschhoek was very close by and indeed it was a three-minute walk to the centre. The centre of Stellenbosch on the other hand was a little way off to the right, but in relative terms on the map, it should have taken us 20 minutes to cycle. An hour and a half later, we came to the turn off towards Boschendal, which on the map promised us a shorter route. So we took it. Mistake number two of the day.

I know. I know. I know all about the old saying that women can't read maps. But this one can. (I learnt more from my geography degree than just the topography and shopping on offer in Norway – expensive beer and no decent shoes). Had the map shown contours, this would have alerted me to the fact that we were heading over a mountain pass and things were about to get a little more difficult.

All I can say is Jim had wanted exercise. And he certainly got it. I, on the other hand, had only planned for a gentle pedal over flat land from vineyard to vineyard, sampling wine, and cheese when it was on offer. The route was earning me major Brownie points with Jim. Of course, I didn't let on that I hadn't planned this at all and just kept pedalling. Jim, I have to say, was fantastic. He did not poke fun at the fact that my complexion changed from fair to beetroot nor that I couldn't pedal and talk at the same time – too much breath needed for the cycling and mine was suddenly in short supply. He motivated and encouraged me so that I managed to conquer hills, at which, I normally would have dismounted after a few seconds.

GO! Read

Why men don't listen and women can't read maps, Barbara and Allan Pease.

The struggle was worth it, and so was the kiss at the top when my breath decided to come back to me. He really was one in a million.

The 15-minute freewheel was our reward for perseverance followed by a bottle of wine and a gourmet lunch in one of the vineyards at the bottom of the hill. The wine succeeded in numbing the thought of the ride back as well as my increasingly throbbing bottom. The waiter, who was a very friendly soul, and aptly named Roly, couldn't believe that we had just cycled over the mountain pass and recommended that we return via the 'normal people's' route. At that moment I could have kissed him, as the dread of cycling back up what we had just freewheeled down just disappeared.

Menu madness

'The more alternatives, the more difficult the choice.'
    Abbe d'Allanival

I have never tasted such delicious pizza as I did that night. Although it nearly proved to be our downfall. We had managed a day of cycling up mountains, misreading maps and finally reaching 'home' without so much as a cross word but everything changed when I was faced with a menu.

Now, I am not going to hide the fact that I enjoy food. But I always have to make sure that I order the right thing. This particular evening, having soaked my nether regions and recovered slowly in a hot bath made bubbly with Head and Shoulders (I was learning to live without the finer things in life), I was ready to tackle the menu at high speed until I saw what was on it. This was, after all Franschhoek, billed as the gourmet capital of the Cape. This wasn't just a pizza place, this was a food pervert's dream. With caramelised onions, marinated anchovies, slow-sun-blushed tomatoes, roasted butternut squash, asparagus tips and a range of toppings that included goat's and blue cheeses I had never heard of. How was a girl to make a swift decision when she had an offer of building her own pizza with ingredients like this?

Jim

"I'll have the seafood pizza with extra garlic and chillies please" I ordered as the waiter came back for the third time (and half an hour after we had arrived) to take the order. What was the problem? I don't need to see the menu – I know what I want. If it is not there, I go for the closest thing. Simple.

Emma

Warming ourselves by another roaring log fire, sitting on a very soft cushion and slowly sipping a glass of Pinot Noir from a local vineyard, I was finally able to make my decision and was rewarded by the tastiest pizza I have ever experienced. A thin crispy base, covered with a fresh, home-made tomato sauce, stacked with caramelised onions, sunblush tomatoes, roasted garlic, marinated sweet peppers and topped with bubbling, smoked mozzarella cheese, a sprinkling of fresh basil and a drizzle of olive oil.

The tragedy, however, was that by the time it arrived, we were both nearly asleep from our exertions of the day, so what we couldn't eat, we boxed up for breakfast, before falling into bed like puppets whose strings had been cut.

Jim

'Respect is love in plain clothes.'
   Frankie Byrne

Rising with the sun we hauled our achy limbs out of bed and with the remains of our pizza, but neither map nor water, we headed for Mont Rochelle nature reserve. On a clear day, Table Mountain can be seen on the walk to the aptly named Breakfast Rock that boasts a fantastic view of the timeless valley, with its orchards and vineyards all in the midst of protected wildlife.

I should have known better. We never did make it to the top despite me having my 'drink water every 15 minutes' head on. Saddle sore and walking like injured stunt cowboys with no sense of direction we gamely (at first) guessed our way to the top before throwing in the towel at about 2,200 feet and 11am. I sat in disbelief. From down in the valley of Franschoek it had only looked like a mole hill.

"Never mind, there are plenty of other mountains to climb, as the saying goes," chuckled Emma, now happily horizontal in the warm purple heather.

"Stupid of me not to bring a chilled bottle of Sav blanc eh? And I should have brought a bloody map too. Sorry." I squinted dismissively chewing on a blade of wild grass in the absence of any tobacco. Well, we were on the dusty trail.

"Look around us, though. It is beautiful here. Stunning."

What did it really matter that we weren't on the top of the mountain? There we were on the side of a mountain, just the two of us, snippets of bird song and the rest, silence.

Go! Think
Take the time out to just be with the moment. What do you notice?

Emma

Climb every mountain

'There is a way that nature speaks, that land speaks. Most of the time we are

Simply not patient enough, quiet enough, to pay attention to the story'

Linda Hogan

The fresh air and amazing views across the whole valley of Franschhoek was worth getting up early for. On our moderately easy climb up the path, there was not a soul to be seen though I did half expect Heidi and her herd of goats to come trotting down the mountain every time we came to another bend in the path. After the bike ride and the struggle of pedalling over the pass, my lungs seemed more receptive to exercise and I was able to talk and walk at the same time for part of the climb. Jim was relieved.

Reaching the top was breathtaking in more than the literal sense of the word. The early morning mist that had lain low in the valley was starting to lift and reveal the beauty of the full palate of colours it had been hiding. Tendrils of wood smoke rose from the occasional chimney and made our senses dance with the enticing smell of log fires. It was glorious to have the luxury of time to stand and stare and be part of the waking of the day as the sun unfolded its warmth. I was filled with pure contentment. I was lucky to be alive.

GO! Think
Through what we perceive to be failure often comes powerful learning and a positive situation to enjoy life. Remember to take the learning with you.

Jim

Our stroll back to the car park led us to a group of German tourists who were struggling to climb over a five-bar gate. Emma flung herself at the challenge commando-style, without a second thought for her manicured nails, vaulting over the top and finishing with a ten-outta-ten landing on the other side. The Germans stood open-mouthed, giving herd-like mumbles of 'Ja, dis is gut.' Like a dork, my reaction was to put a possessive yet proud arm around her. That's my missus. Thank you and good night, Germany. This was a side of Emma I had never seen – the inner child. If only her friends and family could have seen the raw childish beauty of the woman I was falling for.

GO! Think
What does your inner child want you to do?

Emma

Opportunity knocks

'You have to recognise when the right place and the right time fuse and take advantage of that opportunity. There are plenty of opportunities out there. You can't sit back and wait.'
Ellen Metcalf

We had soon fallen in love with Franschhoek and wanted to stay there forever. Not a tough decision to reach when you have great food, vintage wine, far-reaching views and perfect weather. The first night strolling through the town, we had spotted a very interesting property in an estate agent's window. It was called 'Raring to Go' and each day something about it drew us back for one more look.

Franschhoek, which translates as a 'little corner of France', has a picturesque high street of quaint colonial French-style houses and shops with ornate railings, tricolours flying at every available flag pole and an olde worlde charm that is usually reserved for country villages. So after another great lunch, fuelled by yet more wine, we decided that our next 'one more look' at the house in the Estate Agent's window, should be a look at the real thing.

Jim

I have never been over enamoured with the offering of estate agents' windows. It was a shop front, a trader's stand with the occasional must have bargain to temp you. Especially visitors who had that holiday feeling after a couple of litres of wine.

Emma

To our eyes, everything about the house was perfect: a spacious, open plan, single storey four-bedroom home that had very cleverly been split into two. Each sun-filled room had vast glass double doors to the garden, which made it feel like it was part of the interior space. Its prize features however, were the two huge stone fireplaces. They would certainly keep Jim amused for hours as he ran between the two. Exercise and fire building: we loved it.

Raring to go was no understatement, it had tenants in one half that wanted to stay and was being sold fully furnished right down to the tin opener.

Jim

So the place did have a feel good factor about it and aside from the two open fireplaces, my tapping of the walls, stamping on the hardwood floors confirmed this was a well made place in a decent setting. Worth a look.

Emma

We were convinced that this was the opportunity we had been looking for, and which had miraculously found us two weeks into our travels. We talked into the early hours at the prospect of buying a property in South Africa.

Every pro and every con imaginable was examined, from the future of the country, to the perils of taking on a mortgage. Wasn't this what we were looking for, a house that could pay for itself while we earned a living? Jim became frighteningly enthusiastic about taking people walking in the hills and the open fires, while I had my visions of dogs at my feet and cooking gourmet feasts for hungry travellers. I could even convert one of the rooms into a studio and re-awaken my creativity and love of painting. I could even open a gallery.

Jim

Only 5 minutes into our trip of a lifetime and there was me trying to gauge if I could drop any offer by 10 per cent. Worth putting in an offer.

Emma

However lovely it all seemed, there was a sense of uncertainty in the pit of my stomach. Women's intuition, I don't know, but there was something stopping us from making that final step and committing ourselves. The only way I can explain it is the same as going shopping for a pair of shoes and buying the first pair that fits without looking around. What if there was another pair more suitable, better value for money or just prettier? I felt that however beautiful the house was, we really hadn't explored any other options in any other countries. We were prepared to be spontaneous, but were we prepared to buy property in a country still full of troubles?

Jim

I had to admit by the end of our visit that it was the place that we had hoped for and it was us that were raring to go.

Emma

We agreed, much to the agent's disappointment that we would

wait until after the weekend before deciding whether to put in an offer. This way, we would be away from the spell of Franschhoek and able to make a more rational decision.

GO! Think
When you are making a big decision, try to look at the issue from a different perspective. What does it look like now?

Jim
Up the garden path

'Courage is resistance to fear, mastery of fear, not absence of fear.'
Mark Twain

The next day, with thoughts of Raring To Go running through our minds, we hit the rolling hills, on our way to Knysna, which lay, according to the guidebooks, in the heart of the jewel of the Garden Route. Soon, the lush Winelands gave way to the calmer sun-dappled Overberg ranges prompting us to leave thoughts of ownership in Franschhoek behind for the rest of the day and night at least. That night our shelter was to be a ramblers' log cabin in the hills.

Emma
On the way, and about an hour away from our destination, Jim spotted a sign for bungee jumping and literally swerved off the road, waking me from my slumber and screeched to a halt in the car park. Oh no, here we go.

We walked out onto the point of the bridge from where you jumped off, but it all seemed very quiet. No-one around. Maybe it was closed. Relief.

"My palms are sweaty just walking across the bridge," commented a very pale Jim.

"That's a relief, for a moment I thought you were planning to actually throw yourself off," I replied.

If he had gone white as a sheet from just *walking* across the bridge, there was no way he would jump off it. Or so I thought. With Jim's fear of heights, doing a bungee jump was the equivalent of me wanting to sit in a pit of tarantulas.

Jim

I remembered how my friend, Andy, once showed me a video of himself doing his first jump at exactly this spot. I texted him the news that I was standing on hallowed ground and contemplating following in his footsteps. At last, my excuse to use the mobile phone, I was suffering from withdrawal symptoms. *'Wrong bridge, mate. mine was 4 x higher. Don't do it,'* came his reply in seconds. It might have been at baby height compared to Andy's jump, but just walking over the bridge alone made me feel like I'd just necked a double espresso with a red bull float. I shook like a vomiting dog. But the bungee bugged me. It really bugged me. If there was a time to face my fear of heights then this was it.

GO! Think
What fears do you have?

Emma

No way. We picked up a leaflet in the car park and went on our way to find Knysna. It was my turn to drive, but I had no worries about falling asleep. After his near encounter with bungee jumping, Jim was on a high and would not stop talking. The leaflet he had picked up mentioned Blaukran's Bridge bungee jump, the highest in the world and only half an hour from where we were staying. Well, that was just like a red rag to a bull.

Jim

Our log cabin turned out to be another idyll. Shall I bore you? It really was made of logs but surprisingly it came complete with a generous oak-beamed fireplace too that demanded my immediate attention. Bookcases lined the corrugated log-lined walls, which were dimly lit by bracketed lamps and the flicker of the fire. A clear night sky enticed us onto the balcony so we wrapped up warm and huddled close to listen to the nightlife in the forest. A couple of shooting stars later I was dropping off in my rocking chair. It was red neck heaven. All that was missing was a shotgun by my side and my false teeth to chew on.

During our eight-day stay, we gorged ourselves on fresh air, pine forests and early morning mist and breakfasted outdoor on our balcony every morning.

Each day was a sun-drenched day; clear and bright once the mist had gone. You would never have known that this was the start of winter. Not only had Emma found us the perfect location in which to chill out with a view and forest walks, but the Simola 18-hole golf course was less than half an hour's drive away too.

Now, this really was somewhere we could stay forever. As the days rolled on my desire to check my mobile phone and inbox for messages diminished as I started to live in, as the gurus say, the moment Frankly, Franschhoek and 'our house' now seemed a long way away, although we were still considering the offer seriously.

GO! Think

What occupies more of your mind, past, present or future?

Emma

On the rocks

'Sunshine is delicious, rain is refreshing, wind braces up, snow is exhilarating;

There is no such thing as bad weather, only different kinds of good weather.'

John Ruskin

The onset of South Africa's winter only stopped us once. It rained so hard that Jim just had to get the fire going, despite it being four in the afternoon. As the fire crackled, we witnessed dramatic forked lightening. Arm in arm we stood on the balcony and watched. It took us back to childhood power cuts, candles and the art of uninterrupted conversation.The sky turned an angry purple and white jagged tongues of brilliant light, first fired from the gathering clouds, snaked their way to the ground nearby, illuminating our peaceful haven from the advancing gloom of the night. As the thunder gained momentum, it was soon rattling the cabin walls like the big bad wolf.

Mixed-metaphorically speaking, although the fire kept the 'wolf' from the door, mid-storm we heard a strange noise near the back door. Jim as the 'man' went to investigate, fire poker in hand, but was soon calling me over. There, looking very bedraggled, with very large pleading brown eyes and wagging his tail, was a beautiful young golden retriever.

"He must be terrified. Bring him in by the fire and we can at least let him dry off," I instructed Jim.

"Well I don't know. His owner could be looking for him," was Jim's hesitant reply. But I knew that he just wanted that fire all to himself.

After calling the number on the dog's collar, we soon found out that he belonged to the owner of the cabin and was called Shadow. Apparently, Shadow was a friendly soul and as soon as he got wind of the fact that they had visitors he would pop over and keep them company. This was fine by me, I desperately missed my walks with Poppy and Winston and was only too delighted to have some canine company. Jim was not so keen; he loved dogs but was not sure about another male in the place, vying for my attention and a spot by the fire. The brown eyes and wagging tail however won the day and Jim moved aside, leaving his usurper happily curled up in prime position to dry off.

For the next few days Shadow was our faithful wake-up call. Around seven we would hear him scratching on the glass bedroom doors, which led to the terrace. One morning, particularly persistent with his scratching (the dog, not Jim), my very naked boyfriend (Jim, not the dog) went to investigate. As soon as he had opened the door a fraction, all hell broke loose.

Three, yes, three dogs were tearing around the bedroom with wet paws, tails wagging, chasing each other, jumping over the bed in the excitement and barking as though they had just found their voices. This situation wasn't helped by hysterical laughter at the utter shock on Jim's face at the scene of bedlam.

When we eventually returned to sanity by shoving the dogs back outside, we could not believe the damage. Muddy paw prints of all shapes and sizes were everywhere, even on Jim and me. How were we going to explain this one away?

Jim

That night, I had dreamt that I was bungeeing off a hotel in Piccadilly Circus in London wearing my best suit. An ant-sized crowd beneath me cheered and encouraged me to launch myself off the rooftop. In the crowd I could make out the faces of ex-colleagues, university friends and Bo, our old school team goalkeeper. They were holding the kind of safety nets you would find in a circus to save me as I plummeted towards the ground.

That day the dream really bothered me and unlike many

dreams, refused to be forgotten once I woke. It was another sign. Clearly, the world's highest bridge was inviting me to jump off it head first. I was already defying convention, travelling, being spontaneous and living in the moment, so what did I have to lose?

It had become clear during the previous 10 days that our his 'n' hers roles were already ingrained. So this was the perfect time for me to attempt my first braai (BBQ) and exercise my Neanderthal rights around the coals. Em agreed to be fire starter's mate and hesitantly handed me the odd log when instructed, with Shadow expectantly looking on. He was free to roam as he pleased, normally next to any smoking *braai* pit that could offer him a couple of treats.

As Emma returned to her role in the kitchen, I formerly announced my intention to do yet another manly thing: leap off a bloody great bridge. A bemused Emma and Shadow looked on in awe.

"These men and their daft adventures, hey Shadow, what shall we do with them?" she said, feeding her companion the remainder of the disgusting dried meat they call *biltong* that had somehow made it down with us from Camps Bay. I was as stunned as they were.

"Well, you could pass me the wine for a top up for a start, please. I dare not abandon the braai. The steaks are almost done."

"You don't have to do this bridge thing tomorrow, you know," Emma said as she poured.

"I do. I have to do it tomorrow," I replied calmly, flipping over the steak.

GO! Think
Say your fears out loud? How scary do they sound?

Bloukrans' bungee

'I'm desperately trying to work out why kamikaze pilots wear helmets.'
Dave Edison

I was more worried about what would happen to me in biological reflex terms than what would happen in terms of my heart and the height. So breakfast wasn't on the cards that morning. A full stomach was the last thing I needed if I was going to plunge 216 metres (709 feet) off Bloukrans Bridge. Emma drove, offering me one last chance to turn back and put our feet up rather than have them strung up with a piece of elastic rope. With my precautionary tight, dark, Calvin's on, green lightweight trousers and North Face long-sleeved dry-fit shirt, I was good to go and felt I looked the part too. Not that you should judge a book by its cover of course.

Emma

As I drove towards Bloukrans, Jim sat in silence, visibly nervous and reading his book.

"I am sure we can find a copy of the bible, it may be more appropriate" I quipped trying to lighten the atmosphere.

"Not remotely funny" came the clipped reply.

He had temporarily lost his sense of humour. Why Jim wanted to put himself through this, I could only guess and it had something to do with male ego and not being beaten by a friend. Anything he can do...

At first he tried to persuade me to jump in tandem and then settled for me walking across the bridge to see him off. I could manage that couldn't I?

Jim

We drove through the village of Humansdorph, towards the

bridge. Merely driving over it was enough to send me giddy. But I was determined to look cool, calm and collected in spite of my fear. I drank in the scene, as if seeing and feeling it for the last time. The sky was blue, the sun pleasantly making its presence known on the back of my neck and the birds chirping away in the trees, saying, I'm sure, 'What the hell is possessing you to do this?'

The sign at the bungee site confirmed 216 metre depth and that 150kg was the maximum weight they'd permit. Despite filling my face with the country's specialities over the last few weeks, I was confident I'd make the grade and weighed in at just 98kg. I then signed my life away confirming that if and when I died it was my own fault. To cap it all off, they stamped the number 13 on my hand as my identification mark. Finally, just as I was being fixed into the safety harness, they told me that the oldest surviving bungee jumper was 88 years old. What they wouldn't tell me was the youngest one to have been killed!

Even reaching the launch pad, which is a vast concrete slab standing beneath the bridge, is a challenge. A walkway made from a terrifying see-through silver mesh floor with waist high side panels is then covered with a kind of loosely crocheted black net. The walkway, which takes a good ten minutes to cross, has been slung precariously below road height so cannot be seen until you arrive on the threshold. For Emma, the bridge-crossing was just as terrifying as the jump itself. I didn't like it much myself.

Emma

Never mind me wondering why Jim was doing this. When I saw what I had to walk across to get to the middle of the bridge, I nearly changed my mind. No wonder it was called Death Walk – it was nothing more than a cage of chicken wire suspended underneath the main bridge giving the appearance that you were literally walking on air. I physically felt my body rebelling at this;

my legs almost caved way, my breath seemed to have deserted me and my stomach was in freefall down into the bottomless valley below. As I stared in front of me, Jim was striding ahead to the middle of the bridge.

Jim was about to conquer his fear of heights and there was nothing for it but to follow him. It was madness.

Jim

Looking down was a bad idea. I became acutely aware that all that kept me from plunging to my depth was an open grill, the likes of which I was more used to grilling my sausages over on a beach barbecue. But, as with so many scary things we have to face in life, there was only one way to look and that was straight ahead. Clutching the rail I strode as manfully as I could towards the launch site and the sound of the adrenalincreating deafening dance music that pumped out from the mini control tower that lay at my destination...

As I waited my turn the music did the trick. It was intoxicating, and even the sight of the jumpers before me, we were shown on the huge video screen, did not dissuade me. Before I knew it I was sitting on a wooden box, having my ankles laced together with a thick padded red bandage that reminded me of a Sumo wrestler's cummerbund. What happened next was surreal. I was coaxed into a standing position. Two assistants planted their hands firmly in the centre of my back.

They said it would be best if I adopted the crucifix position as I dived off the deck into the abyss. I inched to the end of the platform feeling like I was about to be read my last rites. My Piccadilly Circus dream flashed back into my mind, which then brought on delusions of the comfort of being back in the Dubai office with a mug of steaming coffee in my hand. The moment passed and before I knew it, there was no time to think. I sucked in the air, lifted up my chin and looked as far out ahead into the scenery as possible. This really helped to put my predicament

into perspective and was surely a better option than looking
down.

Go!Read
The Tao of Power, Lao Tzu

Emma
Death walk, fortunately didn't live up to its name and arriving at
the centre of the bridge I was clipped onto the railings just in case
I wanted to throw myself off without the bungee cord. Jim was
bound and trussed up like a chicken on the supermarket shelf. A
strange calm had descended on him, and a manic nervousness
had overtaken me and I was safely strapped on to the bridge and
was going no where.

Jim
The two assistants gave a gentle push and within seconds I found
myself shrieking in an unfamiliar voice:
"1-2-3 BUNGEE!"

Emma
My heart and stomach left me; it seemed to be falling to the valley
floor with Jim. It was a feeling I never want to repeat.

Jim
I felt completely calm. A floating sensation washed over me and
time stood still as I dropped down into the valley leaving my
trailing shout of 'Come on!' behind me.

This was the most amazing feeling of unadulterated freedom
I had ever experienced. All seven seconds of it. I let everything go
and enjoyed the weightless freefall.

I didn't totally let go of everything you understand.
Thankfully, my stomach, managed to hang onto last night's braai.
I'd paid my 500 hundred Rand for the privilege of being uncon-

trollably bounced around like a rag doll. As I gave myself totally to the experience, holding out my arms like a pendulum, the real me came to rest. Upside down a couple of hundred feet up above the Bloukrans river.

But something unexpected happened on the way down. The knot around my ankles slipped a couple of inches. This was it. I was on the way down. There was nothing I could do. A couple of seconds later I was being hoisted back up to the bridge, to a patiently waiting Emma.

Emma

Relief flooded over me as Jim was hoisted back to the bridge. I was so proud of him – he had looked his fears in the face and survived.

"That was spectacular, well done, I am so proud of you – you flew like an angel!" I shouted from my 'safe' seat before struggling free to give him a hug.

Jim was jubilant and very relieved to have survived with everything intact.

Jim

I later discovered that the slipknot was a normal part of bungee. As you come to rest, your mass is at its greatest and the rope slips a little although they rarely tell this to first-time jumpers. What they also failed to tell me was that the jump was free to those who ventured, to do it naked! Now that would be the ultimate feeling of liberation, depending on how cold it was.

GO! Think
Believe you can do it. Focus, self belief and bungeeeeeeee!!!

Emma
Round it or over it, just keep on going....

'Accept the challenges, so that you may feel the exhilaration of victory.'

General George Patton

Time galloped by. With our offer now in place for our Franschoek dream, we had to make one last stop at one last vineyard before leaving South Africa. The Paul Cluuver wine estate in Elgin was our last stop. We were staying in what was once the family house, a small Dutch colonial looking building, which was very welcoming, if not a little isolated and right in the middle of the Estate.

Jim

The man himself greeted us at the gates of his cold, wet estate and took us off on a guided tour of his 120 hectare vineyard. Passionate about his brand, he had pioneered the move to plant grapes in the apple-only farmland. This was a first for this rainy region of Elgin and the speculation paid off. The winegrower, Cluuver is passionate about conservation and sustainable resources. He was the brains behind an initiative to empower South African blacks to look after a sub-label called Thandi.

The idea was to share the land and the end product with them 50:50. In so doing the wine they produce gives locals a slice of what is rightfully theirs. Thandi is now distributed throughout European outlets such as Tesco and bears the emotive mission statement of 'with love we grow together' and I wanted to add to the mantra with 'and a bottle of this wine will certainly help'.

Emma

It was at this point that the weather broke and the rain started. Not with the drama and ferocity of the night at Knysna, but close. As the rain fell, Jim and I somehow found ourselves humming songs from *The Rocky Horror Show*. By evening, we felt brave enough to venture forth and find food. We decided not to go too far and plumped for the nearby tiny village of Grabouw.

The only restaurant that was open turned out to be in the middle of a forest that lay on the edge of the village. So, feeling like we were the next victims of the Blair Witch Project, we set off to find it. Pitch black, pouring rain, distant rumblings of thunder and howling dogs, we eventually found what turned out to be the local pub with all of two people inside: the cook and the owner. A bizarre place, cloaked in silence, located at the end of a dirt track and protected by a barrier and security guard. Ignoring our gut feelings we stepped out of the car. We were hungry.

Realising this was our only food option, we ate a bowl of very hot unidentifiable homemade soup as fast as we could without scalding our tongues followed by soothing hot chocolate, whilst being watched over by the cook. He stood there, with his dark hairy arms folded over his large belly, softly drumming his fingers over his forearm.

"Thank you very much, that was delicious," I stammered. "May we have the bill, please?"

"On nights like this, stick to the path and whatever you do, don't get out of your car, not for anything, not even a body. Drive over it if you have to," he said, slapping the bill down on our table. We paid cash.

We almost tripped over each other getting to the car and rammed the car into first gear. When the security barrier out of the woods wouldn't open, we both sat there thinking that the end had arrived. With the cook's words ringing in our ears, we sat there dumbfounded. We honked the horn. We flashed our headlights only to be met by pitch black and deafening silence. After what must have been only a few minutes, but seemed like hours, a sheepish looking guard appeared from nowhere and released us from our impending doom. We broke the land speed record getting back to the Cluuver Estate and the safety of our little cottage.

With the doors locked, we laughed at what had just

happened, but neither of us slept too well that night.

South Africa had kept all its promises and lodged a few more fond memories for next time. My love affair with the country had deepened and I couldn't wait to be back in Raring To Go. We were on our way to the airport when the estate agent rang.

We had lost the house.

Another couple had beaten us to it. Whilst desperately disappointed on the one hand, we were also both secretly relieved that we could continue on our travels and carry on searching for the next opportunity to find us.

The challenge
Let others lead small lives
But not you.
Let others argue over small things
But not you.
Let others cry over small hurts,
But not you.
Let others leave their future
In someone else's hands,
But not you.
Jim Rohn

Go! Do It:

Take what each day gives you, whether good or bad. These experiences help to build character and shape who we are. How we handle each situation is a valuable lesson in itself whether we are in the comfort zone or not is entirely up to us by the very definition.

1. Think of things that have happened but not as you had planned. Next to each, write down what learning has come from the situation.

2. Live life as though every day is your last.
3. List 5 things you want to do before you die.
4. What actions can you take in your life to make sure you have no regrets if today was your last on earth?

All things happen for a reason, whether it is a sudden death or plans not working out as expected. The reason may not always be clear at the time, but have patience and it will reveal itself. Learn from it, accept it and move on.

'We say that the hour of death cannot be forecast,
But when we say this we imagine that hour as placed in an obscure and distant future. It never occurs to us that it had any connection with the day already begun or that death.
Could arrive this same afternoon, this afternoon which is so certain and
Which has every hour filled in advance'
Marcel Proust

Chapter Three

Flowers and Family

Question time

Emma

'All are lunatics, but he who can analyse his delusion is called a philosopher.'
Ambrose Bierce

Settling down in my economy seat for the eleven-hour flight ahead, I pondered on the last few weeks in South Africa and on the coming months. After South Africa, with its green mountains, fresh air and log fires, Dubai seemed even more like a fading memory of a hot, dusty, traffic-filled desert landscape. But in our quest for what we actually wanted to do and where we wanted to go, we needed to identify what we really wanted from life.

Jim

The working week in Dubai, Sunday to Thursday, normally packed with activity, now simply showed months boldly crossed out with South Africa, UK, France and Peru written in at intervals across double pages. In the back of my pocket diary were some questions I'd scribbled down in 1996, thanks to Marsha Sinetar's, *Do What You Love, the Money Will Follow*. I designed the following questions of my own and have transferred them into every diary I've kept since, but had never taken the time to answer them.

1) What is my ideal day and what does it involve?
2) What do I want in my life?
3) How can I make a difference?

4) What's my life purpose?

5) When do I truly live in the moment?

GO! Read

Find your passion – get the life you live, Jo Parfitt.

Do what you love , the money will follow, Marsha Sinetar.

It was now the time to dig a bit deeper and I decided to answer those five questions. Scribbling them down again, I gave a copy to Emma to answer on the flight to the UK.

So sat side by side, shielding our answers like school kids in a test, we agreed to compare notes back in England. We settled down to find the answers that we hoped would shape our future, I finally put pen to paper and dug deep.

What is my ideal day and what does it involve?

Springing out of bed to bird song, leaving my loved one sleeping and heading out in the fresh air of the countryside with our dogs. My breath escapes with my thoughts into the lush forests, streams, open fields and muddy footpaths. I return fresh faced to our rustic cottage before getting stuck into a healthy breakfast of porridge in the winter, and fresh fruit and whole grains in the summer. Not a trace of the plastic croissant and polystyrene cups, which are surrounding me now in the airport, are in sight.

During the day friends and new acquaintances pop in to share food, laughs and plans as we chew the proverbial countryside fat. There is an open kitchen with a quarry-tiled floor, stable door, Aga and an oak table to seat 12. It's a place that encourages people to be who they are, to be creative, outspoken and free to leave their shoes and worries at the door.

Who was I kidding? I was in American sitcom ville. I picture myself entering the hall to canned laughter.

And cringe. Come on Jim, dream, I think to myself, dream.

Throughout the day we learn from each other, play games,

plan and brainstorm. We're free to take in some of the nearby hill walks and as the sun falls, wherever possible, I get the fire going, play board games and end the day reading a good book.

What do I want in my life?

Simplicity, support and silly amounts of laughter.

I want to have a sense of purpose whilst being part of a community that connects together.

I want genuine passion about everything I do.

I want to be surrounded by inspiring people, whenever possible, whilst being able to be comfortable with moments of isolation and silence. A game of golf a couple of times a week would be a bonus with a smooth, controlled and graceful swing rather than trying to knock the ball into next week.

How can I make a difference?

By not judging people and living instead by the premise of see, speak and hear no evil.

By allowing the things in the universe to conspire and help me find my true calling through other people.

By being comfortable with who I am.

What is my true life purpose or calling?

This is ongoing and will hopefully be revealed as I carry on with life. It is based around people and helping them reveal their full potential by transferring my enthusiasm.

When do I truly live in the moment?

When I'm walking in the hills,

Seated by an open fire,

Reading an outstandingly good book,

Playing games,

When I accept that this is right here and right now.

Looking around me, I had to check that no one had witnessed me writing these things down. My male ego battled to hold onto my macho identity. Still, I realised it had taken me years of procrastination to get round to these questions. And now I had done it, rather than feeling I had achieved something, I felt dread. But something had shifted in my head.

Emma

'Philosophy is the science which considers truth.'
   Aristotle

Answering these questions, however, was no easy task. So, the starting point was to bullet point my answers giving a general overview of the direction I wanted to follow.

1. What is my ideal day; what does it involve?

* Jim,
* A sense of achievement,
* Problem solving,
* Cooking for a kitchen full of people,
* Comfort,
* Warmth,
* Clean bed linen,
* People,
* Long horse rides through forests with my dogs following close behind,
* Exercise,
* Green hills and countryside,
* Lots of laughter,
* Stimulating, challenging, meaningful conversation.

Apart from Jim, these things are not in any particular order.

2. What do I want in my life?

- All of the above, plus:
- Family,
- Friends,
- Good health,
- A comfortable home,
- The means to live comfortably,
- A sense of purpose as well as achievement to each day,
- To help less fortunate people in some way, either through education or by physically helping them to achieve their ambitions.

3. How can I make a difference?

I see this on different levels including:

- Taking the time to make each person that I encounter feel they are important,
- Deeply listening to people and seeing who they are from the inside,
- Giving to people, not necessarily money, but time, heart, skills or knowledge. On a higher level, it includes developing people, help them to see the rich life of possibility and choice that awaits.

4. What is my true life purpose or calling?

Still not sure, but it will involve:

- Contact with people and animals, and loving them. It gives me great fulfilment if I make them smile, like the feeling that it is Christmas Day every day. I believe the happiness that you experience is in proportion to what you give to and feel for others.

5. When do I truly live in the moment?

When I am quiet and still, rather than rushing from one place to another. When I take the time not only to see my environment but also to appreciate it. I want to let go of the past, focus on the present and trust the future will unfold exactly as it should.

These questions presented a starting point for trying to figure things out and working out which direction I want to be facing.

As the plane began the descent into Manchester Airport, I was starting to get a little nervous about what was to follow – meeting Jim's parents.

I wondered what I was letting myself in for during the week 'Up North'. Going through arrivals, I stopped in my tracks as Jim's father was standing waving at us. It was Jim standing in front of me in thirty years' time. Talk about peas in a pod. I had met his younger brother earlier in the year, who could easily have been his twin and now I was faced with Jim in the future. Perhaps they were a family of secret clones?

Home sweet home

Jim

'Home is where you hang your childhood.'
  -Tennessee (Thomas Lanier) Williams

Essentially, Mum and Dad hadn't changed a bit. They both had a few more wrinkles than I remembered, but Dad still had his jet black hair with its left side parting. The only thing that had changed about him was the length of his sideburns. Mum was now the greyer of the two but she still had her big blue eyes.

Thankfully, their humour had remained, as had the sycamore-lined roads of Rossett village, the well groomed flat landscape of my teens. It boasted farms with chestnut trees and grazing sheep on one side, and suburbia with cream-rendered houses and grazing families on the other. Our house had remained as consistent as Mum and Dad with the same 'just hoovered' smell that I always remember, photos of me and my brothers on the landing and the shiny delicate Lladro figurines on the mantle-piece, interspersed amongst the freshly cut sweet peas. But although very little had changed, everything now seemed so much smaller than I remembered.

"Oh by the way" said Marj "there are two huge boxes in the spare room that arrived for you. Heaven knows what you've got in them."

"Great thanks Mum" I replied heading up stairs to start unpacking.

Emma

Jim's mum, Marge, on first appearance, seemed small, timid and softly spoken but it soon became clear that with a houseful of boys to control, she ruled the roost with her quick humour, great cooking and no-nonsense attitude. She welcomed us with cheese muffins that she had baked that morning. It was a typical English summer's day. With the birds singing, we sat in a garden full of flowers and butterflies, sipping our tea on the lawn in typical English country style. I knew I was going to like it here.

Jim

It was great to be back walking with Emma amongst the endlessly blowing wheat fields with the smell of fresh natural fertiliser, breathing in the air I'd previously taken for granted. We retraced my past over bridges, through dense broad-leaved woodland and alongside the river, stopping at the black and white waterwheel of the fifteenth century mill. It was a far cry from the autonomy that foreign-city life brings with it.

As tradition dictated we sampled the local pubs, some of them refurbished beyond recognition. The Golden Lion had gone down the gastro route. Gone were the days of endless stays behind after hours that welcomed a knock on the window from the police who wanted a quiet pint like the rest of us. Despite the change of interior design, the locals remained the same. The same old weathered faces grinned at us across the new, shiny bar, with their friendly pleasantries that really make local pubs. With contributions from Phil the Coal, Jimmy Two Sheds and Tony the Taxi we'd caught up on the last couple of years of gossip in no time. Who needed a local paper when I had this input together with the snippets that mum picked up at the bus stop?

Emma

It took us nearly two days to unpack the DHL boxes as there was little space to put anything. I was wondering why we had brought so much stuff, but hindsight is a wonderful thing. We were off to Scotland for a wedding, so at least one pair of my strappy sandals that had been couriered over was going to get some use.

Jim

A bonny time

'In Scotland, there's no such thing as bad weather – only the wrong Clothes.'
Billy Connelly

Steve and Kelly's wedding was a good four hours' drive away from home. We headed through tight winding lanes, which took us towards Edinburgh, past abbeys, inns and cottages that were barely standing. The endless woodlands of beech, oak and Scotch pine tempted me to go in, camp down for the night, get a decent fire going and sleep on the blankets of velvet, soft green grass. Our base for the wedding was the Corner House Hotel in Interleithan, or 'Interbreeding' as the toothless locals called it.

Steve, Kelly and their lively four-year-old daughter, Ellie Mae, joined us for a cholesterol-inducing dinner of tatties, neeps and Yorkshire pudding. We needed our energy reserves to hit the hills at nearby Peebles Golf Club that welcomed us the next day. The torrential 'Welcome to Scotland' rain came down with a vengeance before we got to the first tee. No wonder the locals looked so dour. We had more rain in those few hours than Dubai had seen in the last five years. With everything slipping and visibility low, it made making excuses for bad shots far easier.

Steve had miraculously been given an exit pass from Kelly to play another 18 holes on the morning of his wedding with a couple of mates. What guy would not want to marry a woman who was that accommodating? I could just picture the vows finishing as Steve's best man hands him his putter rather than the ring.

Do you, Kelly, take Steve and his 14 clubs?"

Marrying Steve was a huge responsibility and a commitment. His clubs were Callaway.

GO! Read

Golf is not a game of perfect. Robert Rotella and Bob Cullen

Emma

Everything I had heard about Scotland appeared to be true: freezing weather, persistent rain and lots of sheep. Thankfully, it also boasted scenery that made you forget any other complaints you may have had. Over the next few days, it continued to rain, with no signs of letting up for the wedding.

On the big day, my lilac linen number provided little warmth, but all was not lost. Set in the grounds of Glen House, an enchanting Borders oasis complete with a hidden loch and a fairytale island, this was any bride's dream and came with a roaring log fire in the library. It was gorgeous and the perfect setting for Christmas. I could already picture it: a tall tree in the hall festooned with decorations and long garlands of holly and mistletoe adorning the sweeping staircase. I considered hiring it for Christmas but the sheer distance from Devon made it a non-starter. But it had however sown a seed.

Jim

Kit Lists

'I will prepare and someday my chance will come.'
Abraham Lincoln

Peru had always been one of the main reasons for uprooting us from our stable, executive careers, so it was difficult to let it go. The site of the lost civilisation at Machu Picchu had been on my list of places to see since geography lessons at school. I played out the scenarios in my head. What was the worst that could happen? We go, we see, we enjoy and return to work? It could be worse. Emma had already proven that she was pretty good at organising a great trip and she relished the challenge of tackling South America without a budget. Her research began in earnest.

While I embarked on my forté of preparing the kit list for Peru, Emma prepared to ensure it wasn't a case of 'all the gear and no idea'. I took Emma to Cheshire Oaks: the largest shopping outlet in the north of England. I knew Emma would feel right at home. With her penchant for shopping however, I felt it necessary to give her some focus, so we devised a system of must haves (rucksack for Emma, sleeping bags and a first-aid kit), nice to haves (spare laces) and not necessary for the trek (handbags, shoes and chocolate). It didn't quite work out that way.

GO! Think

What hurdles are in the way of your dreams? How badly do you want your dreams to become reality?

How will you overcome your hurdles?

Emma

If Jim thought I would be leaving Cheshire Oaks with just a rucksack he had a lot to learn. That place was heaven! The only tragedy was that I couldn't make the most of the kitchen and home-ware stores into which I could disappear for hours. I did however manage to squeeze in a pair of shoes (albeit golf shoes) as well as a carrier bag full of Thornton's special toffee and a few pounds of Cadbury's Roses. Added to my list of shopping, was of course, the rucksack, which had been the whole purpose of the visit.

"This one is great; nice and big and a great shade of purple," I commented picking up the only colourful rucksack on the shelf.

Jim

Why on earth was colour the top criteria when choosing a rucksack? What about water tightness, the frame, durability and breathability?

Emma

Peru had always been one of the main reasons for uprooting us from our stable, executive careers, so it was difficult to let go.

"This one is much better; smaller, more pockets and has a hip strap too," replied Mr Practicality.

Did it really matter that it didn't have a certain strap? The one I had chosen looked better and was far bigger.

Jim

It gets better. The second criterion is the size, so that you can fit more clothes. Erm, so who is going to carry the weight and end up on her back like a stuffed beetle?

Emma
Jim, however, pointed out that if it were too large I would fill it. Ahem. Wasn't that the point? However, I did have a niggling concern that if I did manage to fill a huge rucksack like that, chances are, it would throw me off balance, causing me to land on my back like Kafka's beetle. I think there was a part of Jim that wanted to see me in such a predicament, with legs flailing in the air, just so he could taunt me with the images later. In the end I humbly took his advice. We ended up with one in a lovely shade of grey that was very practical and had all the straps in all the right places.

Jim
She finally saw the light when the shop assistant ran through the selection criteria for a decent rucksack. Thank you.

A warm Devon welcome

Jim

'The moments of happiness we enjoy take us by surprise. It is not that we seize them, but that they seize us.'
   Ashley Montagu

In our hire car, Emma whisked us away from the cattle shed at Exeter airport that wasn't a patch on Liverpool's John Lennon.
   "Do they really drink cider down here and say oo arr?" I asked Emma who was not impressed.
   "You sound like a Welshman when you do that. Anyway, what have you planned for France, Peru and Christmas then?" I asked, changing the subject to something that felt comfortable.
   Emma had been busy over the last few days in Chester.

France was starting to reveal itself as a tour around Provence, part cycling, part ambling. Peru was looking like a six-week tour instead of a charitable six days. Christmas would involve both of our families getting to know each other in a farmhouse just outside Kingsbridge.

We both knowingly grinned as we approached her family's expectedly picture-book cottage with its roses round the door, of course. Emma's mum, June, popped her head around the kitchen door. There were big hugs, big smiles all around and I felt instantly welcomed. June clearly thrived on community life, charity teas, cake stalls and local flower shows. Our very own 'welcome Jim' English tea party was brought out with a range of homemade delicacies that would have given Mr Kipling a run for his money.

June had been well briefed and excused herself for not offering me a cup of coffee, as she'd been warned what a handful I was on the stuff; coffee to me was as good as dispensing a Jekyll and Hyde potion and the fall-out effects afterwards were to be avoided at all costs.

Within an hour I was asleep, mid cup of tea, halfway through a Sudoku puzzle. When Emma's stepfather, Ken awoke, I was reassured that nodding off was a normal reaction attributed to the fresh Devon air.

One beef dinner later, I was fast asleep again, this time in Em's arms.

Emma

A load of bull

'There are two levers fro moving men; interest and fear.'
Napoleon Bonaparte

With the official seal of approval from my family, Carol and David were next on my list to meet Jim. They have been dear friends for over half my life and live on a farm in Kingsbridge with their daughter Abbey, my god-daughter.

Their big, welcoming old stone farmhouse has always been my bolthole and the one place that I knew I could rely on to never change. Being out of the country for such long periods, and noticing how houses had been knocked down and fields replaced by sprawling estates, it was nice to come back to something that was constant. Jim was transfixed, especially when all four of us piled onto David's quad bike one evening to move some cattle.

Go! Read
Sham, Steve Salerno

Jim

How we all got onto that quad bike was beyond me. A good job we were in a position of authority with the size of some of the cows roaming about.

Emma

David farmed a large area of land and was constantly moving his animals from field to field to ensure they always had plenty to eat. And this particular evening was no exception. Having been given our instructions we were dropped off at a strategic fork in a narrow high-hedged, country lane to ensure all went smoothly. Our first job was to stop any traffic coming up the lane to avoid the cars becoming trapped in the middle of 50 cows. No problem so far, as there was no traffic. The second job was standing quietly until the cows came out of the gate, making sure they headed down the lane away from us by waving our arms around and making 'shooing' noises if necessary. In theory, this sounded OK.

Jim

So much for the protective stir of the quad bike. We were left stranded like two lost hitchhikers about to trespass. Then the rumbling of the approaching cattle came.

Emma

As the first few cows started appearing from the field, they were gently nudged into the lane by David on his quad bike. On seeing us standing in the lane, they did as they were supposed to and turned down towards pastures new. So far so good. David then overtook the cows and went to open the next gate to make sure they turned into the right field.

The first car of the evening appeared and on seeing the cows in the road, sat contentedly waiting for the all clear. The last few cows were all behaving themselves so we moved forward to close the gate, which is when we saw him. Grumpy the Bull, living up to his name, was making his way slowly out into the lane. Grumpy was legendary on the farm. He moved at his own pace, would not do anything that he didn't want to and made it known when he wasn't happy.

And here we were, face to face with the bull, with nothing between us for protection, hoping that he would just follow his harem.

Jim

It wasn't even a case of me or the bull. There was no question. I was outta here.

Emma

"Stand perfectly still and don't make a sound," I muttered like the ventriloquist's dummy.

Grumpy stood in the lane, looked down it in the direction of the cows and then looked at us before deciding what to do.

"You may want to find yourself a place in the hedge you can

scramble through in a minute," I continued through clenched teeth.

Grumpy regarded us for a split second too long and my heart sank. Despite seeing the rest of the herd disappear down the lane, we looked an attractive prospect. He took a few steps towards us quickening as he built up momentum.

Jim

"Now what, Em. He's meant to follow the bloody herd. This is ridiculous."

Emma

I was just calculating the best place to scramble up the hedge and haul Jim up behind me, when the car behind us let out a very loud blare of his horn, sending Grumpy in one direction and Jim and me in the other.

Jim

A close call to say the least, the smiling farmer on shining quad bike pulled up 10 minutes too late.

Emma

The visit to Devon was soon over and Jim and I were due to go our separate ways for a few days to see various friends in London that we wouldn't have time to visit together. Jim and I planned to be reunited in London a week later for just one day for an old-fashioned date when we would meet again in the shadow of the London Eye at 11am on 5th September. Apart from the fact that the London Eye had only been in existence for five years or so, I felt as if I was about to take part in a fifties movie. Even this short spell away from Jim confirmed that I had found the person with whom I wanted to spend my future. I had once been fiercely independent, but now doing things alone felt very strange.

GO! Think

Although standing firm is often your first choice, an alternative plan is always a good idea.

What is your plan B?

A date to remember

'I'd rather face failure with you beside me than success with anyone else.'
Jenny de Vries

Our date was better than any movie and seemed to last forever. On approaching the London Eye, I felt strangely nervous. The butterflies flew quickly from my stomach up into my heart as I spotted Jim, looking as handsome as ever, nonchalantly leaning against the wall, making the most of the views along the Thames.

Being a country girl at heart, I was very excited at being in the big city. We seemed to pack a week's worth of sightseeing into a day with not a moment to spare to shop. I had already planned to fly back into London to do our Christmas shopping after Peru so I was happy to leave it for the moment. The Saatchi Gallery, the Dali exhibition, our trip on the London Eye, Trafalgar Square, Leicester Square, Westminster and Covent Garden – we saw them all during the day. We also walked past Harrods, through Hyde Park and down to Buckingham Palace, but not before getting very lost as someone couldn't read the map...

Jim

I thoroughly enjoyed another day when time seemed to stand still. It was then I realized that I realized I wanted to grow old with Emma. Even if she did deprive me of the occasional coffee.

Go! Do It:

How can you get what you want from life if you have not defined what it is you want? How can you get where you want to be if you have no road map?

Take the time to answer the following questions:

What is my ideal day and what does it involve?
What do I want in my life?
How can I make a difference?
What's my life purpose?
When do I truly live in the moment?

Chapter Four

Cafés and Coffee

Jim

French beginning

'Stop thinking in terms of limitations and start thinking in terms of possibilities.'
Terry Josephson

You board a plane and within 90 minutes you're in a totally different place physically, mentally and culturally. This time we Easy-jetted our way from consistently-grey Gatwick to Marseilles: the gateway to the Mediterranean with its thriving port and dazzling limestone cliffs. At the information desk, I attempted to rekindle my schoolboy French and enquired:

"A quelle heure l'autobus departez á Aix en Provence?"

It was the best I could do. The girl behind the counter looked perplexed. After some wild gesticulation, syllable mouthing and finally, resorting to English she understood and passed the tickets for our ensuing journey through the hatch.

"Merci buckets," I replied, attempting to stuff the tickets in the top of Emma's rucksack, practically pulling her back on her heels in the process.

Emma and I marched off hand in hand, into the glare of the Provencale sun. Emma had packed a French dictionary that, as far as I was concerned, like most of the contents of her backpack, was surplus to requirements.

"Look Jim," she argued, "if we only learn a dozen new words a day we'll be practically French by the end of our trip," she tailed off, gazing out from the window of our air-conditioned coach to where the lavender fields of Provence met the rugged mountains of the Southern Alps.

"All the more reason not to bother then," I responded, taking a slug of warm Evian as we sped into one of the many tunnels towards the town of Aix. "We're English and it's the language of the global economy."

Emma

"Aix en Provence is *not* a part of the global economy. It's a quaint French town that encourages the arts, crafts, café culture and fresh produce."

With our lovely grey rucksacks strapped firmly to our backs (and not a stranded beetle in sight) we decided to be proper backpackers and walk from the bus stop to our hotel. Well, that was the plan anyway. I had managed to defy all laws of physics by fitting at least four pairs of shoes in my back pack, together with enough clothes for six months, just in case.

After only two minutes of walking and having to carry my own backpack did I realise the wisdom of packing light. Still, I just smiled, pretending that it wasn't really that heavy. The fact that I had a stiletto jabbing me in one shoulder was not something I was going to admit to.

Jim

The only directions to Les Quatre Dauphins, where we were staying, were that it was near a fountain. In a place that had over 100 fountains, it didn't really help. Despite autumn being upon us it was pushing 28ºC, which by Dubai standards was bordering on winter, although I still had a sweat-soaked rucksack on my back.

Emma

After 20 minutes of what seemed to be aimless wandering, we stumbled on the hotel by chance. We had walked for what seemed to be at least half of the length of France, as Jim tried to convince me that he 'instinctively' knew exactly where he was going.

Jim

When we found it, our room was small and in dire need of a complete makeover. We were perched on the top floor, more of an attic than the penthouse suite, complete with an ancient tower window.

Emma

It was perfect; an old town house converted to a small hotel, with shuttered windows and wrought iron balconies, only a minute's walk from the centre of town and, more importantly, the market. We had missed the market that day as it disappeared around midday, like Brigadoon vanishing into the mists. Still, I could wait.

Jim

The excuse for a bath was barely big enough to wash my socks in and the room boasted just a flimsy wardrobe made from off cuts of unclassifiable wood. There was much more space in our rucksacks than in the wardrobe so our clothes were best left packed. I salvaged my travel journal from the top of my rucksack and jotted down how I felt about this excuse of a room.

Emma

Our cute room was right at the top of the hotel, five flights up ('Inca Trail' I just kept repeating to myself, as we tackled the staircase). Our room was very quiet and looked out over the rooftops of Aix.

Go!Think
When you are lost, how do you find your way?

Jim

Fromage feet

'Swimming is forbidden in the absence of a saviour'
  Sign at a pool in the French Riviera

"What on earth is that smell?" enquired Emma as I wielded the iron I had borrowed from reception on a polo shirt.

"It'll be the drains outside, love. Haven't been cleared for years and if they can't give the place a lick of paint what chance have th..."

"No ... no it's not drains, Jim," she interrupted. "It's right here." She started hovering around me. "It's like the stench of wet leather *meeting* drains."

"We don't even have air conditioning in here," I replied trying to change the subject, 'and anyway, this iron is a waste of time, could you...?"

"Never mind that a minute." Em continued to sniff attempting to locate the source of the smell. It was, she reckoned, my trekking sandals as she wafted them under my nose.

"You're not keeping those stinking things in here are you?" she asked.

"They're not doing any harm. All they need is a bit of fresh air. Look, it's not my feet, I've not had dodgy feet for years."

Emma

I didn't have the heart to tell him that it was his feet and that even the people on the street four floors below could smell them.

Eventually Jim relented and the shoes were relegated to the windowsill. Even the resident pigeons, which had left their calling cards over the years on the windowsill, were clearly not prepared to share their beloved home with such an offending odour.

Go! Read

Men are from Mars and women are from Venus, John Grey

Jim

Market melée

'Perception is real – even when it's not reality.'
Edward de Bono

Having washed my feet in the tiny bathtub, I rescued my sandals from the window ledge and, swilling a measure of mouthwash I spat it into my sandals to give them a better chance of recovery, topping it off with a dab of lavender oil. We were in Provence, after all.

Realising that there was absolutely no need to shave I didn't bother for the first time in years and it felt great. We headed out, winding our way through the maze of streets exploring the sights of the town. As the sun dropped behind the houses the shutters of the patisseries, boulangeries, and charcuteries blended into the stucco walls. Having weaved around the cobbled streets we found our way back to Le Cours Mirabeau to sample the local cuisine. We followed the smells of freshly-baked bread, garlic and roast *poulet*. We settled for a thin crust pizza with chicken, garlic and mushrooms. The Brie on top ensured it was the full French experience. Besides, what's pizza without a cheese topping?

"Do you have to drown it in that Tabasco sauce?" asked Emma as she flooded her freshly baked bread rolls with local extra virgin olive oil.

"Absolutely, it brings out the flavour. Try some," I suggested as I refilled her glass with local red wine.

Shoes and shops

'To eat well in England you should have breakfast three times a day.'

W Somerset Maugham

The endless streets of Aix slowly came to life every morning as the dirt of the previous night was hosed down ready for the day ahead. Emma gave my sandals one *very final* go with the mouthwash before we went out in search of local coffee and fresh croissants.

Wedged into our plastic chairs in a nearby café, we could observe a succession of chain-smoking locals, who had come in for their first drink of the day. They chatted with friends at the bar before going off to work. Some of them appeared to work in the market where their trestle tables displayed an array of local produce, including fresh fruit and veg, garlic tapenade spreads and local cheeses.

Emma

Jim ordered his first coffee for several weeks. I tried every reasonable counter argument, but as he pointed out, no self-respecting Frenchman would have his morning croissant without a good cup of coffee in which to dip it. Straight away, I pointed out that he was *not* a Frenchman. But he did have a point. And who was I to deny him the French experience? My mind had already worked out that if I gave in I could always lose him for an hour or so amongst the market stalls while the effects of the caffeine hit wore off.

With the first sip and dunk, I held my breath, waiting. But I was surprised and amazed that there was no effect whatsoever. Was it too soon? A delayed reaction? Ten more minutes of calmly watching the proceedings of the morning and still nothing. Hallelujah! I am not sure who was more pleased, Jim who was now relishing the thought of coffee and croissants every morning, or me for not having to cope with the fallout. This

French way of life was becoming more appealing by the minute.

Go! Read
A Celebration of Olives, Carol Drinkwater

Jim

One cup of coffee became two as we watched the market-stall traders, often alongside or selling out of their vans. Conversation accompanied most transactions with the money passed over almost as an afterthought. This timeless ritual appeared so effortless. This was French soap opera on tap and we enjoyed watching it unfold around us.

"It's so inspiring here, don't you think?" asked Emma as she tracked a couple of mongrels hopping into the back of a market trader's Renault Clio amongst stacks of punnets of end-of-season strawberries.

"You'd soon get into the swing of it, the art, fresh fruit, vegetables, the essence of cultural life. Some of the great artists got their inspiration here and I can see why."

"Inspired to sit and dip giant croissants in their coffee all day?" I replied pensively rubbing my stubbly chin.

"I'm still flabbergasted on how this French coffee has no effect on you. Amazing." Emma tutted as she raised her hand with the customary "L'addition s'il vous plait."

Go!Think
What is your inspiration?

Aches and pains

'From now on I'll never leave the room without saying how much I love you.

This takes a long time. Maybe a pat on your butt will do.'
Homer Simpson

Our time in Aix pressed on. So too did my belly on my belt as the debauchery of South Africa, the UK and now France started to catch up with me. I was experiencing similar aches and pains to those that had confined me to bed back in Dubai and I found it increasingly difficult to resist the coffee every day. As well as my energy, our spending money was also beginning to dwindle as we prepared to move on further south to spend ten days discovering the secrets of Provence by bicycle. This demanded a basic level of fitness; more than was needed to walk between coffee shops and boutiques. I needed inspiration and an end game.

"Let's just take our time then and not push it," suggested Emma, not wanting to complicate things. I couldn't bear the thought of doing nothing though so I took to stretching first thing in the morning before leaving our room. If nothing else it would help cancel out the croissants I was about to ingest. My mental stimulation had come from rubbing my new, academic-looking ginger goatee and Googling in Aix's smoke-filled internet cafés.

Mid-Google it occurred to me that Emma and I could be in it for the long haul. Maybe the next stage of commitment was what I was looking for? I'd had plenty of practice at the relationship game over the years but this was different. I was completely myself when Emma was around. And that was a first. Suddenly I was thinking marriage.

I had always wanted to travel and reach Machu Picchu. They say love isn't conditional and it wouldn't be, but I knew that not only was Emma 'the one', but that Machu Picchu was 'the' place to ask her to marry me. I was becoming increasingly sure that Emma was the one with whom I could take on the world.

I began researching the suitability of Machu Picchu as a place in which to 'pop the question'.

"You go off and enjoy the shops, Love," I threw out at Emma, in a quest to get some research time alone. "See you in an hour."

Emma

Normally I would be rubbing my hands with glee at the prospect of time alone to shop, but because there was obviously something he was keeping from me, I lost all interest in the shops, becoming very interested instead by my emails.

"No, it's OK thanks, I have a few emails I have to sort out for myself," I said trying to fool him into thinking I wasn't interested in shopping.

But Jim wasn't buying this and with gentle persuasion I left reluctantly to mooch around the shops trying to kill time before I could return to investigate just why he had become so secretive.

Jim

I became the bleary-eyed, round-backed e-customer whilst Emma was the bright-eyed, lively master of the markets. I was free to make my lists and fold them away in my minimalist wallet while Emma was free to squander all the euros she wanted.

Emma

I was not in the mood to explore what Aix had to offer when there were far better secrets to be revealed in the Internet café. It was suddenly far more appealing than a free rein to shop. What was he up to? I decided it was time I found out.

Jim

My surfing time was beautifully uninterrupted until Emma unexpectedly returned to the café to find me angling my terminal away from her prying eyes rather less subtly than I had intended.

"What you up to then?"

"Bit of web searching, Love," I replied, clearing my throat and clicking on the refresh button to get back to the Inca trail web page.

"Looks a bit suspicious to me. You on one of those dodgy sites?"

This escalated into our first e-based argument. I wouldn't show Emma my e-history, or the inbox on my account.

Emma

I was shocked to my core that Jim could get so defensive over a little Internet history – what was he hiding? What did this mean for our future? Our relationship to date had always been open and honest and now, suddenly, it had changed.

Jim

My lack of openness was new ground for us but an internet café wasn't the place to drop down on my knees and propose. It would have to wait until I was 100 per cent sure that I wouldn't be cursed by the Inca gods for asking for Em's hand in marriage. What if she said 'no', or 'yes' or 'I need time to think about it'? I needed to rehearse my response to all three.

"I'm planning part of our trip. Don't worry about it," came my truthful answer.

"I've sorted the Peruvian Secrets outfit. Have some faith in me and trust my planning, Jim," came the justifiably irate answer.

"I'm only checking out what ruins to see in the time we have. We can't possibly do it all."

Emma

I was still not convinced, but this was going nowhere so retail therapy beckoned after all.

Go! Think

There is a balance between keeping a secret and deceit. What is your balance?

Jim

Change

Going to Machu Picchu to propose was the ultimate place for me followed by a simple, hassle free wedding. The question was where, when and how? Maybe up in a hot air balloon, mid deep-sea dive or on the eighteenth green of Nad Al Sheba golf course? Simplicity was the key and the thought of a sun-kissed beach ceremony suddenly appealed.

Ignoring the tip-tap of the keyboards around me I shut my eyes and tried to imagine the scene. The picture of suits on the beach didn't appeal; formality defeated the object and was hardly free and easy. Maybe shorts and sandals (new ones). With my beer belly and a double chin? Preferably not. A healthy glow, white linen attire and splashing around as the waves lapped at our feet. Perfect. I knew of just the place.

An ex-colleague, John was the eternal expat, having experienced most parts of the Gulf for the last four decades. Enjoying all the privileges that came with his lifestyle slowly took their toll on him. Five years ago, after a second heart attack, he followed doctor's orders and put his life on hold before it came to a permanent end. He bravely tucked himself away for a week of fasting and detox at the Spa Samui in Thailand. It proved to be his literal life-saver.

Having had irrigation twice a day and followed a fast for eight days he left the Spa 10 kilos and several thousand Baht lighter. As he returned to normal, bobbing around in the sea off Thailand like a cork and learning to eat Pad Thai, a chance meeting occurred. An investment opportunity presented itself to him at the unspoilt Fisherman's Village of Bophut. The last strip of beach was up for grabs along with planning permission. Fast forward to the present day and John's modest, Thai-style boutique hotel now sits in tranquillity, amongst the lush palm trees and the golden sands. It was worth a look on Google if nothing else and a toe-in-the-water email.

Simplicity was the key. Nothing against our far-flung friends and family but we'd struggle to afford even an average UK wedding. Finance aside, the thought of pledging our love down the aisle of a cold church that briefly reunited family only seen at weddings, funerals or christenings just didn't appeal.

Emma

Wacky Races

'If winning isn't everything, why do they keep score?'
Vince Lombardi

With our week in Aix at an end, our cycling tour was due to start at Draguinon; an hour's train ride east of Aix. The sunshine and blue skies were left behind, we were met with dark clouds and the threat of heavy rain. This was not my idea of fun – I am a fair weather cyclist. On the first evening we were introduced to the rest of the group at the team briefing, which was almost drowned out by the noise of the rain on the roof.

The group cycling from the same point included a young Scottish couple who had managed to cram a ten-day holiday into just four – surely missing the point. Would *they* have time to smell the flowers, I wondered, or even notice them as they peddled? There was a mother and son from Australia with a frightening level of fitness, which meant I certainly wouldn't be *their* cycling companions. And finally, apart from Jim and I, there was a pair of Norwegian sisters in their late fifties who were both recovering from illness and had decided to take time to smell the flowers before they found themselves pushing them up. Their respective illnesses had made them re-evaluate what was important in their lives and spend time with each other.

GO! Read
Chasing Daylight, Eugene O'Kelly

We would all be cycling independently, setting our own pace for the day and meeting up each evening at the hotels. We could start when we liked and it was up to us how often we stopped for a beer. That sounded great to me, not worrying about keeping up with anyone. With the pain of our South Africa bike ride still in the forefront of my mind (or rather bottom), I was not too keen to repeat the experience. was looking forward to going at a gentle pace exploring parts of France that were off the beaten track, that might one day become our home.

Jim

After a few drinks to get to know the other couples who were up for the challenge we were introduced to our cycles. For the next ten days with a couple of road bikes, panniers and puncture repair kits we were set to discover England's favourite French *département*.

"Get familiar with your bikes, finish the puncture repair workshop and we'll be ready to wave you off in the morning," instructed Aaron as he helped one of the groups squeeze their inner tube into the housing of the front wheel.

The beauty of this leg of the tour, full credit to Emma, was that Aaron, our Mancunian, pony-tailed tour guide, transported our rucksacks between each guesthouse. All we had to worry about was taking in the sights, staying on the bikes, navigating our way and ensuring our panniers stayed full of red wine and bread.

"So, enjoy your tour of Provence, It's an 08:00 start tomorrow, remember. Here is our emergency help line: use it if you need to and we'll come and get you," said Aaron as he handed out business cards to the group.

This really was cycling for softies. Or so I thought.

"Fat chance of us needing that," I told Em as I laid out my

cycling shirt, disturbingly tight Lycra shorts and white socks ready for the next day. "That's only for the unprepared, those with all the gear and no idea."

My cycling skills soon returned after a humiliating start. In front of the hotel in full view of the rest of the group, I attempted to pedal off in a rigid fifteenth gear only to seize up the chain and end up on the gravel surface of the car park. I'd mixed up my first and fifteenth gears and tangled up my legs and arms in the process.

Aaron leapt to my aid and picked me up like he would a fallen rucksack. Emma cried into her hanky with laughter and I tried to hide my red face. Maybe they'd give me stabilisers or a support Renault Clio with flashing hazard lights bringing up the stragglers?

During one coffee stop (Em was now allowing me just one per day) we enjoyed the company of the mother and son team from our group. She was a fit fifty-something called Suzie from Australia with her even fitter Lance Armstrong-like son, David. They were on the French leg of a six-month tour of Europe. Cycling was their life and she had originally planned to do the around the world thing with her busy executive husband.

Sadly, he had died the month before they were due to embark on their dream trip. So he never lived to see the places they talked so much about experiencing together. Luckily, David had agreed to replace his dad to ensure that his mother enjoyed the trip that she'd worked so hard for over the years. If there was ever any justification needed for our mid-career sabbatical then this was surely it.

We were determined not to miss out on a single dream.

GO! Think:
What is your dream?

Go! Read

It's not about the bike, Lance Armstrong

Emma

The rain that had threatened to soak us the previous night had not materialised except for a few light showers that were very well timed when we stopped to get a freshly baked baguette for our first picnic. With the tapenade from the markets in Aix, a Camembert that had ripened nicely over the last few days, both our mouths were watering at the thought of the feast that awaited us later in the day.

Jim, keen to make up for time lost on our uncertain wanderings earlier in the day, wanted to pick up the pace a little so that we could relax over lunch. If there was no race involved, why were we in such a hurry? The countryside that we were cycling through was everything and more than we had expected; quiet vineyards, sleepy country villages, pine forests and tree-lined lanes. The locals, after their shock at seeing two Lycra-clad Brits whizzing through their peaceful lives, seemed happy to see a bit of life and sent us on our way with a smile and a wave.

When our stomachs dictated that it was lunchtime, we found a quiet spot in the woods that would also give a little cover from the rain showers that kept threatening to turn into a downpour. Midway through our feast of bread and cheese, we were rudely interrupted by another couple from our group whizzing past with a smile and a wave. The super-speedy Scots had caught us. That was it. Disgusted at being overtaken, Jim packed everything away and set off in hot pursuit. All thoughts of a quiet siesta, as is customary in this part of the world, had vanished.

A little later, we saw their bikes chained to railings in one of the villages, where they had obviously stopped for lunch. It took all my powers of persuasion to stop Jim letting down the tyres so that he could secure an even better advantage. This was turning into the Wacky Races, and I had visions of me (Penelope Pitstop) and Jim (Dick Dastardly), becoming outcasts and being thrown off the tour.

We were not passed by any other cyclists that afternoon and so got to our destination hotel, safe in the knowledge that we had 'won' the first day. We soon discovered the victory to be hollow as it became clear that the other cyclists were not staying at the same hotel. They were on a slightly different tour and had different accommodation for the night. This information was the best piece of news I could have heard. It meant that there *really* was no competition and that the next few days of the cycling would be done at leisure. We could take the time to stop and smell the flowers.

Jim

Tyred out

'Once, during prohibition I was forced to live for days on nothing but food and water.'
WC Fields

A hung-over start to each day took its toll, especially half-way up a particularly steep hill first thing in the morning, which was arguably the best part of the day and would have been best enjoyed sitting outside a café with a coffee under a shady lime tree. Despite the idyllic places we were lucky enough to be cycling through, I wasn't getting the most out of it in my red-eyed state. 'Never again, Em,' was my standard response when offered a beer at lunchtime. On a couple of days, we took the liberty of stopping at the halfway points to sneak into a wood and sleep off the excesses of lunch. With only the drifting butter-flies and silence to accompany us, we had just enough time to relish these precious moments.

GO! Read

A Year in Provence, Peter Mayle.

On day five, when lying in a bloated state following a large lunch, the idea of a new challenge came into my head. I vowed aloud to stop drinking for the remainder of the cycling tour. "An egg is an egg, Em," I said as I plaited some dead strands of grass together.

"Eh?"

"You know. As the French say, *un oeuf is un oeuf.*"

"You're talking in riddles, Jim."

"Enough is enough, Em, I've had enough of drinking. I'm not touching a drop until we've finished this cycling malarkey."

"Don't put yourself under that kind of pressure, Jim," Emma puffed as we set off on our bikes towards some ancient abbey that advertised home-brewed beer and wine.

"I'm sick of putting my bike tyres under 100 kilograms of pressure let alone my vital organs. You drink away to your heart's content," I said as I raced ahead.

Leaving booze alone is far easier when you feel in good shape. I was on top form as we climbed up to the pure vastness of Lac St Croix. The hills were fine too and so my first real test came when I refused a beer when we stopped at a café one morning. Emma ordered a shandy and wiggled her eyebrows as she wickedly informed me that they had thirst-quenching Stella on draught. I'd earned my beer, as always, but this time I declined and had a peppermint tea. This was a battle and far harder than the morning's cycling as I pretended to enjoy my unusual beverage. Focusing on the view whilst other people enjoyed their wine, I reminded myself that in five days' time I could drink all the alcohol I desired. The week would be over.

Emma congratulated me with a 'well done' that I repeated to her when she pedalled hard and made it up the steepest of hills to our digs overlooking Lac St Croix. It was the most serene place

I'd visited in my life, with not a jet-ski or expensive boat anywhere in sight. Tomato juice was hardly fitting for the occasion but I managed a couple of sober Scrabble wins as we sat on the terrace sharing a spectacular sunset. My liver and kidneys were now on vacation as well and were already enjoying the break as I enjoyed a good night's sleep.

Go! Think:
What good health habits do you need to get?

Secrets of Provence

'Our patience will achieve more than our force.'
   Edmund Burke

As we got into our cycling and good-night's-sleep routine, our fitness improved enough for us to tackle the mountainous climbs up to the village of Tour. Tour is known locally as the 'village in the skies' and aptly reported by the other cyclists as torture. But it was well worth the effort. We enjoyed a bird's-eye view of the rolling terraces that epitomised Provence.

Wear and tear on the bikes had however started to show and Emma's back brake failed and a spoke came unhinged. On our final couple of kilometres up to the hotel she sounded like a tumble dryer with a spanner in the drum. Emma suggested that it might be best if we called the helpline.

"Join the dreaded incompetence club? Moi? Never. Get yourself a nice relaxing bath, Love, and I'll fix the bike," came my defiant reply.

Emma

There was not much I could say to change his mind when he had his 'Mr Fix-it head' on. I did not want to think about the state of the bike after Jim's 'repairs'. A hot bath sounded like a far better option than watching him take the bike to pieces and not remember how the pieces fitted together again. Why is it that men have to prove themselves and cannot ask for help?

Jim

Dusk came and as Emma headed off into the room I routinely locked our bikes together and to the bike stands. In my keenness to get my hands on the noisy spoke and unstick the brakes I rushed the lock-up drill in the process, half turning the dial as it clicked into place. I'd somehow managed to snag the lock. It was neither in its housing and fully locked nor was it free for me to take the lock off. It was well and truly stuck.

No matter how much I tugged at the thing nothing happened. Even our guide couldn't help and suggested calling the local *gendarme* to bring the bolt cutters. It was a Catch 22 situation. Either I had locked the bikes up for the rest of the trip or it was time to call help in and adopt drastic action. Other guests at our digs came out to try and help. This was beyond embarrassing.

"Weren't you the guy who fell off his bike at the car park?" smiled one of the Italians who had been at the briefing, and had now caught us up on our tour.

"Yep," I replied sheepishly.

None of the assembled group could understand how I'd managed to get our combination lock in such a state. Then Emma, having had a good hour in the bath, came down to see what all the fuss was about.

Emma

After a hard day's cycling, I wanted to stay in the bath all evening, but felt that I should go down and support Jim in trying to fix my bike (or was it because I wanted to check that I still had a bike to ride?) It wasn't fair to leave him down there alone, so off I went.

I know that Jim enjoys playing to an audience, but when I saw about ten people crowded around the bike and hearing their laughter, I dreaded what was waiting for me.

Jim

"I thought there'd been an accident. What's happened? Did you fix my bike?" came Emma's voice from the back of the crowd that had formed.

"Not exactly," I replied as I tugged away at the lock.

"Allow me. This needs a woman's gentle touch." Offered Emma, pushing her way through the ensemble.

"We've been here for an hour, Love, no job for you." I said dismissively, but relented and passed her the lock. What could she do that we couldn't? We had been at it for the best part of an hour.

Emma

Apparently, Jim had not even started on repairing the bike and each of the male guests had lined up to compete to see who would be the first to break the lock - without any success.

Jim

Much to my disbelief, within less than a minute she'd freed up the lock and with a cocky grin went back inside.

Emma

To this day I have no idea how the lock came free, but with one touch the two pieces fell apart.

"Well, that's that fixed. Is there anything else that needs doing?" I asked, desperately trying to keep a straight face.

And when there was no answer, I silently and carefully locked the bikes up, looked around the sea of male faces with their mouths all agape, and went inside for dinner.

Go! Read

The rainbow of liberated energy, Ngakpa Chogyam

Game, stretch and match

'Figuring out our gifts in life is part of our journey to becoming enlightened human beings'
Allison Dubois

Over the week, we were in our element. The exercise was making us feel good and as a result, we both had cut down, and eventually given up, on the alcohol. The effect it had was amazing; better sleep, which meant far more energy and waking up with the sun. We hoped we could trust ourselves to keep it up.

The cycling came to an end all too quickly, but what a spectacular end it was. The last stop was a place called Tour, commonly known as the village in the sky. There was a gruelling climb up an everlasting hill, but as I felt ready to enter the Tour de France at this point, it was not a problem. The trip organisers had certainly saved the most breath- taking views until the end. By the time you had registered the beauty of what you were seeing, the top of the hill had arrived. And the view was spectacular; an endless patchwork of olive groves, ploughed fields, stone walls and hedges with a scattering of tiny, terracotta-roofed villages stretched far into the distance. The autumn sunshine provided an additional touch to the already colourful scenery and the heady scent of the wild rosemary filled the air. What we saw and experienced that day was very special.

The view from someone else's shoes

After ten days of near solitude on quiet country roads and sleepy villages, Nice was quite an assault on the senses. There was the bustle of traffic, crowds of people and a faster pace of life to that we had just experienced. We soaked up everything, enjoying the contrast to the last three weeks.

There was one planned excursion on our agenda for the next four days: one that could jeopardise our coffers – the casino.

But before risking it all we enjoyed a gentle stroll along the 'Promenade des Anglais', savouring the mild evening and the intoxicating sea breeze. It was reminiscent of elegant Brighton in its Victorian hey-day; a very different feeling from that of Aix-en-Provence. A much more cosmopolitan city that made it feel somehow less 'French' than any of the other places we had visited.

We were in a world of our own, enjoying the whole experience of Nice's seafront in the evening. So we were more than a little surprised to find that we were not allowed into the casino when two rather mean looking bouncers barred our way. With my heart leaping, I jumped to the conclusion that they thought we were under-age. I was flattered...

Realising that we had to be smart, we had made an effort, but I then remembered Jim had insisted on wearing *those* sandals.

Jim hadn't thought that his footwear would be an issue, but the two bouncers took one look at his feet and stopped us. At this point it is tempting to say it was because of his feet being on show and frightening people, but the gesture was followed by an American drawl.

"Hey, sorry guys, but men are not allowed to come in wearing open-toed sandals, that's the rules," he apologised.

"What about women then?" came Jim's quick thinking reply, "Would they be allowed in wearing sandals?"

"Sure, there's no problem there. They have nicer-looking feet," came the reply, trying to make light of a rule that he obviously thought was absurd. Before I had time to register what was going on, Jim's sandals were off and he was in the process of prizing my delicately beaded slippers from my feet.

"You cannot be serious?" I uttered realising what he was intending.

"Why not, this is sexism at its best? If you can wear sandals then you wear mine and I'll wear yours. Shame you haven't got bigger feet though."

The sight of Jim's feet in my lime green, beaded silk shoes was enough to send the bouncers into hysterics.

"Nice try, but it's more than my job is worth. You might want to try the gay club down the street though. They may let you in."

There was nothing else to do but try the next casino down the road. This time we were successful.

Following a celebratory post-casino drink, we thought a gentle stroll back to the hotel would finish the evening beautifully. What happened next was enough in my mind to make sure that from here on in I should be in charge of any maps or activities that involve directions.

GO! Think
What is more important to you; the taking part or the winning?

Why can't this man read maps?

'If you don't know where you're going, it doesn't matter which way you go.'
Lewis Carroll

On leaving the casino after doubling our money, Jim insisted that we turned right, convinced it was a short cut, but soon went very quiet when the streets we were walking through became unfamiliar. It was midnight, on a Saturday in a big city, hardly the best time to start experimenting with short cuts.

Jim
My sense of direction had abandoned me but I was not about to admit it. I had absolutely no idea where we were, nor was I was

not going to ask a waif and stray 'ou est l'hotel?' I just wanted to get back to base, and quickly.

Emma

As the streets got darker, so did the people. The more we tried to correct the mistake, the more lost we became. Jim, becoming more and more concerned for my safety, kept reassuring me and kept a tight hold of my hand. My other hand had a tight hold on my crystal (as had become my habit in anxious moments), hoping it would offer me the same protection that it did in South Africa.

Jim

Two drunks argued on a nearby bench and a prostitute guarded the street corner ahead. This was one tour of Nice that I did not expect, the further we went, the more convinced I was that we would not see the hotel until the next day.

Emma

Dimly lit, foreboding streets seemed to be waiting for us at every turn, together with increasingly shady characters. I became very concerned about our safety, but thought it best to keep quiet as commenting on an obviously worrying situation was not going to help matters. I just prayed yet again, that my guardian angel was on duty that night.

After a good 20-minute walk, we eventually came across the main road that led to the station from which we could thankfully find our hotel. However, to get to the road we had to walk past a sex club, which was advertising all sorts of services.

Jim

Where the hell was our hotel? The only thing on the horizon was a neon sign for a sex club. My heart sank until I realised it was the same club we had passed as we left the train station when we arrived in Nice. I was back on track to find the hotel but did not relish the thought of Emma walking past such a seedy joint and suggested we take a short cut. One look from Emma and I changed my mind and walked past the club.

Emma

His grip tightened, maybe for fear that I may dart inside. We eventually found the hotel and never have I been so glad to see the inside of a familiar room. To go from the opulence of the casino, through the back streets of Nice to be faced with people earning a living any way they can, was a shock.

It certainly gave us a reality check on the privileged world in which we had lived for the past three weeks. I wondered if any of the people that we had passed on the streets that night had ever stopped to think about what they *really* wanted from life and how they could get it. Getting lost had highlighted to me yet again, the importance of knowing where you are heading in life.

The contentment of being in France was quite overwhelming. It was not because of any luxury item, fancy way of life or material gain, but rather an appreciation of small, simple things.

Go! Read
The Monk Who Sold His Ferrari, Robert Sharma

Go! Do It:

Don't always be in a hurry to get where you are going; take time to find out what is important along the way.

1. What are the 'essentials' in your life that you will always try and make time for?
2. What do you feel is important but often neglected?
3. Remember, simplicity has richness. What are the simple things that you value in your life?

Chapter Five

From Shampoo to Shaman

Jim

Back to base

'Adventure: the pursuit of life.'
Daniel Roy Wiarda

As we arrived hand in hand at John Lennon International airport in Liverpool, the 'Above us only sky' strap line was pushing its luck as it was hammering down with rain. Above us, in fact, there was only cloud and we dived for cover, dodging holiday-makers and their loaded trolleys, as I spotted Dad's green Peugeot. The family taxi was bang on time.

Emma

Tropical rain, when I am in a bikini or autumnal rain when I am beside a log fire is fine. Freezing cold rain while standing outside Liverpool Airport with a heavy rucksack is not. I was just thankful it wouldn't be too long before I found myself in warmer climes again: I had a week's holiday planned with my mother in Majorca.

Jim

'Golf is a game that is played on a five-inch course – the distance between your ears'
Bobby Jones

"Quick, chuck your stuff in the boot. Bleeding rain," squinted Dad as he squeezed the car boot shut on our weathered rucksacks.

"Welcome back to paradise. Do you know, I'd just finished cleaning the car this morning before it decided to pour down? Typical Sunday weather," he joked as he flicked the windscreen wipers to overdrive.

"If it doesn't rain it pours," I mouthed in anticipation, as we passed a huddle of cyclists sheltering under a Merseytravel bus stop covered in Liverpool Football Club graffiti. Dad rarely had a bad word to say about anything, with the exception of the rain. He hated it with a passion. Having been completely denied it in Dubai, I welcomed it. Emma couldn't see the attraction or understand why I was hunched over the computer leaving her to catch up with Sunday soap opera T.V with the folks.

I needed my Google fix and to finalise the options for changing Emma's surname to Wheat on a Thai beach and the plan for Peru. My time online had been drastically cut since our French internet café experience and a busy inbox awaited me with a couple of confirmation emails sent in no time. The Samui Spa in Thailand would indeed be happy to accommodate us in mid January before the wedding, with a Buddhist blessing afterwards. I confirmed the dates whilst throwing Emma a white lie about having had to suffer the indignity of an empty inbox. It was all set.

Emma

Jim was could hardly wait to get on the Internet when we returned, but I had given up asking him why. I just had to hope that it was not a gambling addiction that meant we would end up broke.

I had other things to worry about. I was blonde and loved it. But, whilst it brought me attention and gave me an excuse to get away with my 'blonde moments,' I wasn't so sure I wanted the attention in the north of Peru. So with a little trepidation I sat in the chair of a salon in Chester and set about explaining what I wanted.

Jim

The local golf course was basic by Dubai standards but was 100 per cent natural. Set around the dense woods bursting with chestnut, acorn and sycamore trees. The local farmer had spotted an opportunity and adapted his land to good use. He'd also recycled local waste from the treatment plant to scatter onto the greens.

GO! Read
Golf is not a game of perfect by Bob Rotella.

"Bit of fresh air for us today, Son," commented Dad as he sarcastically screwed up his nose.

"Bit of news for you today, Dad," I replied, as I took my three-wood from the bag trying to ignore the pervading stench of waste.

"What, you're going to take your dad for a pint after we've finished?"

"Possibly. I'm going to ask Emma to marry me."

"Right. A pint it is then! Now hit your ball son, your Dad's going to give you a whopping."

With the gauntlet thrown down I did what most golfers do when they try to hit a ball too hard. I shanked the shot with all my might and watched the ball pathetically trickle into a near by ditch.

"Now then son, keep your mind on your game. That, as Aristotle once said, was directionally poor."

Emma

Two and a half hours later, the dye was washed off and my horrified look said it all. The hairdresser admitted that it was 'a little' on the red side.

Another hour and a half later, having asked her to tone it down, the second and then third lot of dye was washed off, and

I was left looking like an autumnal patchwork. In all fairness, the hairdresser had done a good job and I was secretly pleased with the result after the initial shock of looking like an exploded tomato.

Jim was fantastic and seeing my face full of uncertainty, must have read my thoughts the minute I walked through the door. He very gallantly made lots of reassuring noises that men don't usually make. Who cared if men really do prefer blondes? This man thought I was gorgeous, and to me, his was the only opinion that counted.

GO! Think

Listen to the opinions and advice of the people that are closest to you. They will have your best intentions at heart, but evaluate their advice. Is it for your development or their preference?

Jim

Emma looked gorgeous and her excitement increased as she recalled how Laura had been right. The Angel card I had been dealt in Dubai had not only featured a dark-haired woman but also a mountain range in the background. Emma had kept a photocopy of the card and challenged my skepticism by producing it out of her rucksack. I couldn't argue with what I saw and genuinely complimented her on this new look despite cries of "Really, do you really think so? If only she knew just how uncannily accurate this was with the proposal I had in mind. I just hoped that we would complete the Inca trail for my faith in Angel cards to be confirmed.

Emma

Girls' talk and lots of it

'A memory is an etching that time has engraved upon your mind.'
Richard Brown

I was now ready for a week in Majorca with Mum. But the realisation that I was leaving Jim behind left me with a bittersweet feeling. My rucksack was packed with all the things I knew I wouldn't be taking to Peru; a hairdryer, toiletries, two bottles of perfume and five pairs of shoes, and lots of very impractical clothes that were ideal for the beach (although I was only there for seven days). This was my last chance to pamper myself for a while.

After meeting up with Mum at Palma Airport we were soon at our hacienda-style hotel overlooking the beach. Our room had an enormous balcony, where I was looking forward to planning Christmas over a few bottles of chilled white wine at sunset, after a leisurely swim in the sea. This was all very well in theory, but there was one thing missing; the sun. Each morning we got out of bed hoping to be able to take out our swimsuits. But we managed a measly two mornings of sunning ourselves before the clouds and cold drove us inside again.

I believe things happen for a reason. Mum and I were not meant to have sun that week as there were far more adventurous things to be done. We hired a car and drove through the countryside, which was peppered with olive groves, orange trees and dusty ploughed fields contained within low, ancient stonewalls. We explored the old stone villages inland, discovering picturesque squares filled with colourful, bustling markets where the locals happily went about their daily lives. We had time, without any interruptions, to talk and enjoy each other's company, to reminisce about childhood stories that had lain forgotten in our memories.

GO! READ
Girlosophy, Anthea Paul

Although I was missing Jim, Mum made an excellent companion. We shopped, we talked, we laughed, we explored. After dinner each evening, regardless of whether it was raining or not, we would have our coffee and a large Drambuie on the terrace and talk about the day, before retiring to our room like giggling school girls hoping in vain for some sunshine the next day.

By the end of the holiday, we did not care that the sun had stayed away because we had the most wonderful time building irreplaceable memories together.

GO! Think
Building memories is a great pastime. None us of know how much time is left.

How do you make the most of every moment?

Kit lists, compasses, wet wipes and sun cream

'We always hold hands, if I let go she shops.'
Allan Pease

Back in Chester we put the final pieces of our Peruvian jigsaw together as our trip was now only five days away. While I was organising myself as best I could, I wasn't quite prepared for Sergeant Major Wheat's level of organisation.

The morning dawned with a blue sky and sunshine that surpassed anything Mum and I had seen in Majorca. And Jim leapt out of bed, enthusiastically demanding to see my kit list.

My what?

Jim

"Proper preparation and planning prevents poor performance" I reminded Emma, rubbing my chin in concern at the collection of irrelevant fashion accessories laid out on the bed.

Emma

He explained that as we were going on an expedition we should put together a kit list so that we knew exactly what we had with us and were prepared for anything. OK. True, our trip to Peru was going to be tough: it included camping in virgin jungle and a three-day horse trek away from all civilization to visit a mausoleum 250 metres up a cliff face, not to mention a 7 day Inca Trail hike over the mountains. So, I agreed that this required careful planning and packing – but with a shopping list I could handle.

Jim

Her priorities on her kit list were so wrong in my opinion; handi-wipes and talc made it to the top of her 'must have' list. While a penknife and compass were at the top of mine. We'll see whose comes in handy.

Emma

I realised that I would not be taking my hairdryer on this trip, but there were still a few essential issues to consider: I needed toiletries to last two months, a wardrobe for all weathers to fit into one rucksack, and appropriate shoes (I guessed stiletto sandals were out).

Jim

Another shopping trip was called for if we were to be taken seriously on the trail.

Emma

So, we marched out for a day's shopping in Chester where Jim made a beeline for the Army and Navy Store, while I opted for Boots. Enough said. I closed my eyes to everything that I would be leaving behind and decided on five essentials: toothpaste, sun cream, deodorant, lavender shower gel (that would double as shampoo) and my packets of wet wipe cleansers, which I knew would come in handy. I'd leave Jim to buy things like ropes and compasses.

Jim

Army and Navy had everything we needed - Spare batteries for the maglite, a map case, wicker underwear and altitude tablets. All essentials for the trip.

Emma

Proud of my purchases, I set off to meet him. Jim stood there beaming, surrounded by bags from the Army and Navy store.

'Are you about to enlist?' I enquired

'What do you mean?' he beamed.

'What you have managed to buy in such a short time would put any girl to shame,' I told him, hoping that he would remember his new-found shopping skills when it came to Christmas.

Jim

As Emma finalised her Peruvian packing my inability to hold a straight face went unnoticed as I gamely sat on the top of Em's rucksack, as bid, so she could wrench the straps tight. She'd didn't look too pleased that there was little room to fit an extra pair of shoes along the way.

Emma

Peru's all

'I'm not afraid of crashing when I fly , my secret is just before
we hit the ground, I jump as high as I can.'
   Bill Cosby

When we finally made it to the airport it was pouring with rain,
pitch black and freezing cold, but I didn't care. Gone was the
girlie mentality of hair, make-up, nails and shopping. In its place
was the fearless adventurer. I was going to encounter much more
than a few spots of rain in the next two months. And I was ready.

   We landed in Lima around lunchtime having flown
backwards in time, gaining nearly half a day. We were met by
Daniel, our squinting chain smoking Peruvian Secrets' rep.

   'Take care and leave valuables in the safe. Don't drink tap
water, eat any salad or swallow when cleaning your teeth. You
might get cholera. Happy holidays. Mugging Westerners is
Lima's national sport,' he concluded.

   'Oh, really? I'd heard this was a friendly city,' said Jim hoping
to make light of it for my sake.

   'We are a really friendly bunch, that way we find out just how
much money you have and then relieve you of it,' answered
Daniel chuckling, with Jim reluctantly joining in earning a
'would you like a cigarette' offer from Daniel. Before we had
even landed, I suggested to Jim that instead of keeping all of his
money in his immaculately ordered wallet, he should keep only
the smallest amount in there, with a few other bits scattered
throughout his pockets. He reminded me that not only had he
travelled by himself many times without being mugged but also
that he had been a Sergeant Major in the army cadets and no one
would dare come near him. I conceded that all he had to do was
wave his smelly sandals at them and they would soon beg for
mercy. This was going to take a little more gentle persuasion.

Even with Daniel's warnings, Jim thought he was invincible.

The hotel in Lima was far better than I had imagined and I was only too happy to sink into the nice crisp linen sheets for a quick nap to try and adjust to the fact that it was mid-afternoon and my body was telling me it was nearly midnight.

Jim

While Emma unpacked, I ventured out in search of some drinking water. Wandering around the iron-barred grimy and chaotic neighbourhood with clenched fists by my side, I felt like I was in a vigilante computer game, but with only one life. A stray dog barked and battered car horns beeped as locals beckoned me inside their bars for a Creole experience that involved either a pole or a roulette wheel. Eventually I found a tiny shop where I handed over my Peruvian *sol* through the wrought iron gates in return for a couple of litres of carbonated *água minera*. The tired lady, with her varnished native skin and tightly combed black hair managed a *gracias señor* before returning to her battered radio in the corner.

Emma

Twenty minutes later Jim still wasn't back and I was nearly beside myself with worry. Having all sorts of visions of having to call the police to put out a missing person's bulletin, I went to find the passports. They were missing too. That was all I needed. I now had visions of being stuck in Peru, with no Jim and no passport. Just as I was picking up the phone to call reception, Jim walked through the door smiling, unable to understand why a cushion was flying through the air dangerously close to his ear.

GO! Think -
What impact does your ego have on your life or someone elses?

Jim

Down to Earth

'He is the happiest, be he king or peasant, who finds peace in his home.'
Goethe

Next stop was a village and the home of our host, Herbert, a disgruntled German Civil Engineer who having had enough of Europe, opted for Peru a couple of decades earlier.

'Peru is a country, like any modern society,' he explained very matter of factly.

As we bumped 80 dusty kilometres towards Herbert's home, in his dented air-conditioning-free pickup truck, we passed endless barren plains with irrigation ditches strewn with litter, political billboards and giant sandy mounds, which were allegedly ancient burial sites.

Emma

Herbert's house was one of the most amazing buildings I have ever seen, not because of its architecture or fixtures and fittings, but because it was built completely from mud. Even the vibrant ochre and terracotta colours that I initially thought were paint, turned out to be different coloured earths. All lighting was provided by either kerosene lamps or candles.

GO! Read
The Barefoot Home: Dressed Down Design for Casual Living, Mark Vassallo

Jim
In Peruvian terms this was the home of someone with a privi-

leged existence. Herbert was an ecowarrior, occasionally reliant on a small generator (switched on for special occasions, such as preparing dinner for us), water drawn from a well and every variety of cacti imaginable.

Emma

We had been warned that there was no electricity at the house and no mains water, but the food and wine were astounding. Herbert's adopted Peruvian son, Manuel, was a master in the kitchen and created meals that would have put most of the restaurants in Dubai to shame. What's more it was all achieved in candlelight, with no modern gadgets. It was astounding what they created from the most basic ingredients. We took so many things for granted in Dubai, things that, in reality, we could so easily do without.

This was an amazing place. It was very tranquil, set around a beautiful garden. I slowly began to relax and forget my fears of mugging. That was until Herbert dropped the bombshell.

'Be sure to make sure you shut your bedroom door at all times,' he said, 'even if nipping to the bathroom. We have some pretty ugly spiders here and they love to take refuge inside.'

'What kind of ugly?' I asked suspiciously. I knew this place had to be a little too perfect to be true.

'Oh they're not really that bad, just baby tarantulas,' he replied nonchalantly. That was it, all illusions shattered. Red wellies, red wellies, red wellies, I thought to myself. I would be OK as long as I kept the door shut. Jim however, as it turned out, appeared to have been born in a barn, constantly leaving it wide open. Why had I never noticed this before?

That night on the way back to our room, I sent Jim on first as the advance party, in case any webs had been spun across the path. We didn't find any webs, but we did find one of the offending creatures cowering at the side of the gravel path. On closer inspection, I was beginning to wonder what I was so frightened of. It was a baby tarantula, and seeing the size of its bulbous body I realised not only why Herbert had said to keep the door shut, but that there was really no way that thing would fit under the door. The hypnotherapy must have been working; by now I would normally have been a screaming banshee racing down the road trying to put as much distance between myself and my eight-legged enemy as possible, stating categorically that I was not setting foot in that place again.

When our time with Herbert was almost at an end, he felt we could not leave without a visit to his neighbour, the local witch doctor, known as a shaman. Thinking this would be quite spiritual in the middle of a forest at sunset, I couldn't have been more wrong.

GO! Think
How do your phobias affect your life?
What difference would it make if the fear no longer existed?

Jim

Which Doctor?

'That old black magic has me in its spell,
That old black magic that you weave so well.'
    Johnny Mercer

We handed over our 50 sol at dusk the next evening and entered a semi-circle of high cheek-boned locals around a fire in a clearing in the woods, wondering what the hell we'd let ourselves in for. We were asked, through interpreter Daniel, what we would like from the menu, as he shakily read us the Sshaman's specials:

1) See the shaman's table
2) Guinea pig scan

3) Egg reading
4) Crystal fire
5) To be de-flowered
6) To be rejuvenated

As the options sunk in, the shaman gave us a guided tour of his offerings that were spread out on a blanket. Alabaster saints, parts of animals, crystals and special potions were all for our use. We wondered whether this was such a good idea after all. I certainly wasn't having any deflowering going on, shaman or no shaman. Em, being a pet-lover, enquired what a guinea pig scan entailed. It involved rubbing a live guinea pig over the body to pick up energies. It is then split open to reveal any human ailments reflected in its bloody organs.

GO! READ
The way of the Shaman by Michael Harner

Em's jaw dropped. 'I'll pass on that, thanks all the same,' she replied shaking her head.

Folk medicine is one of Peru's oldest cultural traditions, practised by shamans or healers. Their powers of foresight and ancient knowledge made them interpreters of their culture's religions.

I opted for the crystal treatment. Rubbed over your body, wrapped in foil and thrown into the middle of the fire the crystal was retrieved 15 minutes later for all to see. I stood helplessly in the middle of the circle of locals, arms out and eyes closed like a sleepwalker. Daniel the interpreter told me the news. 'You are a traveller,' was the shaman's first observation as he examined the crystal's cremated remains. I couldn't argue with that. More prodding followed as he began to blow ash from the now solid-ified crystal.

'You visit high and low places and have some small worries,' he said as his wide eyes reflected the flickering of the flames. Fair enough, Machu Picchu was on our list.

'Your worries are only small,' he repeated.

'You, *señor*, are well-centred, decisive and will be successful. Now open your eyes.'

The shaman drank a slug of what looked like neat alcohol, spat it out on the back of my neck and shook his arms and legs like a puppet on strings. Herbert explained that ingestion of this *Ayahuasca*, distilled from an Amazonian vine, apparently builds a bridge with the past and helps reconstruct painful experiences that can be treated by healers. It gave me a wet neck and made me smell like I'd been on the sauce since lunchtime.

Emma

Rather than adding to the mortality rate of guinea pigs, I opted for the egg diagnosis. Not knowing what to expect, I was a little surprised when the shaman held the egg in his hand before skilfully rolling it over my entire body with the flat of his hand and cracking it into half a glass of water.

Just like Jim, he spat alcohol over the back of my neck, chanting some incomprehensible words and staring long and hard at the egg floating in the water before proclaiming with a flourish:

'Ella es normal.'

Was that it? After all that I was normal?

Seeing how up close and personal the shaman was getting to me throughout, Jim seemed a little edgy. 'How do you feel?' he enquired on the way back to the house. 'Spiritually cleansed?'

'No,' I replied, 'I feel like I have had an egg rolled over every part of my body only to be told I am normal.'

It was certainly the spiritual experience I'd expected.

Go! Think

What does 'normal' mean to you?

Altitude attitudes

'The poor long for riches and the rich for heaven, but the wise long for a state of tranquility.'
Swami Rama

We caught a bus, which had been hijacked the week before, without a hitch (or hijack) and headed for Tingo. The road, or rather lack of it, was a gravel dirt track with what must have been ten thousand ruts every kilometre. It was an honest introduction to what we could expect from now on.

Jim
Our base for three days, in the 2,000 metres-high valley of Tingo, was a wooden hut without electricity. The fresh air and home-cooked, home-grown food made up for it. At this low altitude we both had slight headaches, which I am delighted to report, allowed my coffee ban to be temporarily lifted. Maybe it was the air or the disturbed night bus ride, but whatever it was we slept a good ten hours after our first taste of the Andean village life.

Emma
We needed to find some horses that would take us on the three-hour trek up what seemed to be a very steep mountain to the ancient city of Kuélap. This could not be pre-booked as there were no phones here, let alone fax or email. There was one satellite telephone in the village for emergencies only. There were no tourist companies here: this was the real deal and everything was done by word of mouth. As the village comprised only four hundred people, they all knew each other anyway. The beginning of the horse search started and ended with the lady who worked in our hostel. She knew a man, who knew a man who owned some horses we could use.

Following our local stable owner, Daniel, Jim and I trotted off, following patiently through the village, looking like something from the Wizard of Oz.

It turned out that we were being taken to her house to see her horse in the meadow. But not only did we get to meet the horse, but also the grandmother washing their supper of beans in the stream, the daughter, Lizbet with a new puppy, which sat devotedly at her side, the pig, the donkey, the chickens and the ducks. The daughter walked two miles to school everyday, the wife had a job and the husband worked on the farm to provide food for the table that the grandmother happily cooked.

To our Western perceptions, with no electricity, no running water, apart from the stream at the bottom of the garden, and a basic two-roomed house with earth floors, they were deemed to be poor. But really, they were one of the most contented families we had come across. The horses looked fine and so, a deal was struck.

GO! Think
What gives you the feeling on contentment? What actions could you take to increase this in your life?

Jim
Saddle up

'Dangerous at both ends and uncomfortable in the middle'
  Ian Flemming

Horses frighten me. Not so much to stroke or to sit on but the thought of standing behind one and receiving a kick to the head terrifies me. If there is a mountain to be scaled, I'd rather climb, pedal or cable car my way up.

I was clearly too big for my excuse of a horse. It was more like a donkey. Daniel, our guide, assured me that my 'untrusty steed' could take my 100kg weight. I wasn't convinced. If I stretched my legs out they touched the ground on either side. And the horse had a mind of its own during the three-hour trek, which took us over ravines, through rivers and up to a finger-tingling 3,000 metres.

Emma

'In nature there are neither rewards nor punishments, there are consequences.'
    Robert Ingersoll

We tried not to make any comment to the effect that Jim looked more like a drum on a pea than a rider. I'm sure that if he had taken his legs out of the stirrups and worn roller blades he could have helped the horse up the hill. Jim settled into it however and even got the hang of making his horse go faster, strangely enough by blowing kisses at it.

The narrow mountain track that we wound our way up, together with the 300 foot drops on each side went unnoticed by Jim and his fear of heights. The views as we reached the top just got better and better until at one point we had a 360 degree view of the mountains and the narrow valley below. This was our first taste of the Andes and, I wondered if it could get any better.

Jim

We found ourselves perched on a limestone ridge above the Utcubamba Valley, Kuélap, which, in its day, must have been an impenetrable fortress. This imposing stone citadel, 700 metres long and 110 metres at its widest, is surrounded by huge walls and sheer cliff faces. Having reached this site, I could appreciate why cowboys walked the way that they did. I was hurting and Vaseline was straight in at number one on my things-to-buy list. Local relief came from a very unexpected source. Daniel rummaged around in a side pouch, grabbing what looked like loose leaf tobacco and began to chew.

Within 30 seconds we were all trying to pack as much coca leaf into our mouths as possible.

"Now, leave it in for a good 20 minutes," advised Daniel as we chewed this apparently legal staple of local culture. Within that time my saddle-sore hobble had been replaced with a confident cowboy swagger as we walked around the ruins.

Daniel proudly told us how this was one of the most advanced civilisations to develop in the tropical jungle region of Peru. Kuélap took 200 years to complete and millions of cubic feet of stone were used to keep out the Spanish conquistadores. Its strategic location between the Marañon and Utcubamba Rivers, both long tributaries of the Amazon River, protected it from being devastated. It was also safe from tourists as very few ventured up this far, particularly on horseback.

Descending back down into the smoky valley of Tingo was far easier than the ride up until the torrential downpours moved in. Welcome to the Andean rainy season. We passed over ravines and meandering rivers to be greeted by the gap-toothed, weathered-faced locals gathering up dry bundles of bright yellow sweetcorn.

Emma

The horses, realising they were homeward bound, sped up a gear or two. This was fine on the flat, but as we approached the hairpin bends, still with 300 foot drops, Jim's horse decided to have a little fun.

He was obviously the hungriest of the horses and was fed up at being called a donkey. All of a sudden he streaked out in front, playing a game of 'chicken' with Jim, insisting on going right to the very edge of the track on each corner. Realising there was nothing he could do, Jim just closed his eyes and hung on. By this time, both Daniel and I, with tears streaming down our cheeks, had nearly fallen off our 'trusty steeds' laughing. Jim, was fast disappearing into the distance as his horse went faster and faster.

'You can get the beers in then, as you'll be the first back,' I called after him. Strangely, I didn't get a reply, but heard him mutter 'bloody donkey' as he rounded the next hairpin bend.

Jim

Back at base, we devoured homemade pizza with a Peruvian topping of sweetcorn and mushrooms. Greens were pretty much off limits for us *gringos* as Daniel assured us that we didn't have the stomach to take them. To make up for limited fare I foolishly wolfed down what I thought was a handful of sweetcorn kernels, not realising they were in fact ridiculously hot chillies. My lips and tongue swelled up, my eyes watered and it took me a good half an hour to return to normal.

Emma

It had been a long and tiring day. I didn't care that I stank of horses, my nails were broken, my hair 'au naturel' and that I hadn't worn make-up since leaving the UK. In fact it was a huge relief. It wasn't that I just didn't mind. I loved it. In Dubai, or any city, you feel compelled to make the effort to put on your best show and groom yourself to perfection. In Dubai, my job demanded it and it was shocking if I didn't conform. Here, I felt there was no façade to keep up; you were accepted for who you were, not what you had. It was like a breath of the fresh air and air that I wanted to continue breathing.

My moment of reflection passed and one truck ride later we were at Lemeybama, base camp for one of the most important discoveries in Chachapoya archaeological history.

Go! Think

Where and how do you experience a metaphorical breath of fresh air in your life?

Happy on horse back

'Challenges are what make life interesting; overcoming them is what makes Life meaningful.'
Joshua J Marine

Much larger than Tingo, Leymebamba boasted a town square, cement-covered roads (of sorts), a hotel, a museum and even a restaurant (albeit in the front room of someone's house). On the one hand we were taking a step up the ladder of civilisation, but two steps down again as we started our three-day trek on horseback to find the mausoleum that once housed the 219 mummies discovered several years earlier.

We had been briefed that we were to take only basic essentials to fit into a day pack. A day pack? I had already got my essentials for Peru down to a 52-litre rucksack, but I managed to strip down even further to a dry change of clothing, my toothbrush and clean underwear. I was ready.

Jim

We'd packed as light as we could for the next four days. Our soap would double as hair gel, toothbrushes were snapped in half and the toothpaste tube we had left was rolled up (or down) to pocket size.

Our transport for the trek was a pack of horses (15 hands plus, we were told) that would carry us, our kit, our food and our water. I didn't doubt it. These horses were huge and this was a different ball game altogether. Oh dear.

Unlike the horses, our two weather-beaten guides, had the combined height of seven feet, and I wasn't convinced they would be up to the job. They pitched up with hessian sacks of food, team wellies and a blue tarpaulin each.

GO! READ
The Mammouth Book of Wild Journeys, Jon E Lewis.

'Are the tarpaulins to keep the horses dry, Daniel?' I asked as I tried and failed to mount my horse.

'No, they are waterproofs for the guides. It is all they have.'

Emma
Cowboy Jim looked like he was kitted out for a fancy dress party, as a cross between the Lone Ranger and John Wayne. It's a shame he didn't have their cowboy grace when it came to mounting his horse.

Jim

Trottathon

'What we see depends mainly on what we look for.'
Sir John Lubbock

Once I had figured out which foot had to go in the stirrup, one of the guides patiently waited to hoist me up. It might have been easier to lower me on via a crane. Heave-ho, 1-2-3 and up. With a push from behind I was a good 12 feet tall and patted my horse to assert some form of control. I slowly relaxed into the saddle as we proceeded onwards and there was nothing else I could do but smile and go with the horsey flow. Within an hour of winding our way up to over 3,000 metres and reaching the valley, the heavens opened.

Out came our ponchos and the horses' tarpaulins. We were soon leaving civilisation behind along with bedraggled, thin cacti, lush valleys and fierce running streams. The torrential rain made for slippery surfaces with streams of water constantly forming around us. Steep narrow roads became perilous dirt tracks as we squelched on regardless.

Emma

I wasn't sure how long we could put up with these conditions. Wind, rain and freezing cold meant that I had lost all feeling in my fingers and toes. Two hours later, we stopped for lunch under a hanging rock that was the only dry place around for miles. We ate dry crackers and cheese – and they had never tasted so good.

Jim

We needed the energy for the ride. It was hardly leisurely. The only time we dismounted was on the steep, slippery downhill slopes. Uphill, I was determined not to fall off. I grabbed my steed's mane as we made our way up a series of rocky slopes. The horses made the odd unexpected slip and holding the reins politely was simply not enough. How these animals and our guides, who were relentlessly walking alongside us, kept going was beyond me. But by now, we had thankfully bonded, as the twists, turns and sheer drops my horse subjected me to demanded there be trust between us.

We were 4,200 metres up with heavy rain beating down on us as we experienced a huge drop in temperature. Emma's extremities were still numb as we headed towards freezing point. Both of us were struggling to suck up the air at this height as we tried to focus on the job in hand, wondering when the hell this leg of the trip would end. In an odd way it really stirred my soul. The rawness of the landscape, man and machine (well, horse, porters and supplies, anyway) formed like dots on the vast Andean landscape. The challenge of the experience, and the fact that we were among the few who were brave and stupid enough to have ever attempted it was exhilarating. 'Now then, this is more like it, *this* is Peru,' I remarked, casually glancing over my shoulder with the reins in one hand and pointing at the overpowering scenery.

'No shit, Sherlock!' replied my bedraggled girlfriend as she sucker-punched me for stating the bleeding obvious.

As we headed over the barren ridge down to the 3,000 metre mark the site of vegetation welcomed us as we hit dense sub jungle. Over streams, dipping in and out of dense woodland, and admiring the overwhelming rock faces, we really began to enjoy the ride. The rain subsided giving way to the welcoming sight of our digs for the night. What appeared to be an abandoned wooden hut was in fact a ranch hand's house.

Emma

'Fatigue is the best pillow.'
Benjamin Franklin

The cabin was incredibly basic to a Westerner's eye, but to the Cloud People (named because they lived at such high altitude) who had made it their home, it was sophisticated.

Our bedroom turned out to be a stable with a dry straw platform for a bed. After the day we'd had, this was like heaven. We were given a candle to act as our light source (no fire regulations here) and shown the location of the bathroom, which consisted of a hole in the ground, modestly shielded by a split plastic animal feed bag as a makeshift curtain and a bowl of rain water in which to wash. The candlelit bubble bath would obviously have to wait until we returned to Leymebamba. Putting on dry clothes, we headed to the kitchen, or rather cooking area. There was not a fitted cupboard, sink or cooker in sight, yet we had one of the most delicious meals on our travels so far. The fire on the floor in the corner was the 'cooker' and the 'sink,' the ground outside.

The way of life here amongst the Cloud People was incredibly basic and being here felt like we were living a history lesson. Despite a life of what we perceived to be hardship, they seemed far more content than some of the successful folk I had met in

Dubai with their huge villas, fast cars and housemaids. We had much to learn from these people, which was very humbling to acknowledge.

Even though I knew that when deprived of basic comforts in life you appreciate what you have, the last few days had really highlighted it for us. Being content with what we have and not always longing for more was liberating for the soul. A simple life can often be as rewarding as that full of luxury; the trappings of life often add stress rather than comfort.

Go! Think;
How true is this for you?

Jim

I vaguely remember being fed and watered and finally crashing out on a bale of hay as I fell into my sleeping bag.

Emma

Indiana Jones and the mausoleum of mummies

'Joy lies in the fight, in the attempt, in the suffering involved, not in the Victory itself.'
Mahatma Gandhi

After the deepest sleep that I can ever remember, we were awake at sunrise, ready for the next part of the trek. This time we were facing it without the horses. Whilst I was not looking forward to the six hours of walking and climbing that lay ahead, my bottom was thankful to have a day off.

The walking was never going to be easy, but being at altitude made it almost impossible. Five minutes after walking up an almost vertical hill, my lungs almost exploded with exertion and I was desperate for my horse, sore bottom or no sore bottom.

Jim

I was so glad to be walking unaided, at my own pace in my own boots through the forgotten jungle of the Andes. The horses deserved a day off, and I was looking forward to the burn in my lungs from a bit of honest exercise.

Emma

My lungs were soon forgotten as the Lagunas de Los Condores came into view. A huge, dark and forbidding lake, with vertical cliffs as a backdrop, lay like a menacing dark pool below. Our guides pointed out the orange cliff paintings that marked the site of the mausoleum that was the goal of our trek. To get there we had to descend to the lake and cross it via a temporary log bridge, and cut through the jungle, to find the ladders that would take us 250 metres up the cliff face to the tombs. At this point it started to rain heavily. If being at the log cabin was like living in a history lesson, this was like taking part in a very real Indiana Jones movie.

As the guide chopped his way through the virgin jungle with a large and lethal looking machete I followed close behind like his faithful assistant, shimmying over slippery logs perilously perched across the narrowest part of the lake, scrambling up cliff faces with the help of tree roots and edging across ledges being pounded by waterfalls. I was soaked to the skin, splattered with mud but fuelled by growing anticipation of what we were about to see.

Jim

I was itching to get my hands on that machete. It was a serious bit of kit.

Emma

Eventually the rock overhang came into view, and seven rickety, homemade ladders later, we were standing on a ledge that had not felt a drop of rain in hundreds of years. This was obviously the reason for choosing such an inaccessible place to bury the dead. The ledge protected everything around it from the torrents of rain that were now falling.

Standing there surveying the scene below, we began to realise just what we had achieved to get there. The experience of getting here had far outweighed what we had come to see.

Several skulls that littered the ledge, along with the brightly coloured wall paintings were all that remained of the sacred site. The sense of achievement of being one of only seven hundred people who had visited this site was enormous and quite an emotional experience given all that we had gone through to get there.

Jim

A wave of accomplishment flooded over me as we stood perched on a ledge with our guides and the abandoned skulls and mummified remains of a by-gone generation.

Emma

Climbing up was one thing but getting back down was going to be quite another. The rain stopped, which helped a little, and it was easier than we thought until Daniel slipped and disappeared down a very steep muddy slope. Holding our breath, we peered over the edge, not quite knowing what to expect, but there, like some cartoon character that had just fallen over a cliff, was Daniel clutching on to a very small branch that he had managed to grab on the way down. Seeing his grinning (or was it grimacing?) face reassured us that all was well, or at least would be once we had pulled him back to safety.

'Can you please wait until the end of our trip to throw yourself over a cliff, you have a few more menus to translate for us yet,' we quipped, relieved to see him hauled to safety. He took it all in his stride and ambled on smoking as he went.

Jim

The guides told Daniel that it was rare to have gringos like us during the rainy season and were particularly impressed with Emma. So was I. She hadn't uttered a single complaint on the ride, didn't mention the lack of hairdryer or a warm bath and made do with a sleeping bag and a bale of hay for a bed. She'd make it to Machu Picchu, I was sure of that. The stamina of our guides amazed us too. Their ability to keep us at ease, motivate, feed and water us whilst getting stuck themselves was humbling. Management schools could learn a thing or two from these guys about true team leadership.

GO! Think

When you push yourself to the extreme of your personal limits what does it reveal about your true self?

Emma

Return to civilization

'Contentment is not the fulfilment of what you want, but the realisation of How much you already have.'
Anonymous

Like a reward for our persistence over the last few days, the sun shone brightly for the return journey back to Leymebamba. It had been an exciting few days, not only in terms of physical achievements but mental ones too. Six months earlier I could not have pictured attempting half of what we had just achieved, but now I was ready for more.

The last few days had certainly made me appreciate everyday luxuries such as the hot running water we have come to take for granted. What I will always remember is the look on the faces of the people who were our hosts at the cabin: looks of constant peace, contentment or satisfaction. Whatever it was, they were happy with their life.

With our trek at an end, we now headed further north in search of more jungle adventures.

Go! Do it:

It is quite often the journey that teaches us not only important lessons in life, but about ourselves too. Sometimes it can be very surprising to find out just how resilient we are and what we can achieve when we are not prepared to give up.

1. When you dig deep and push the limits, what do you discover about yourself?
2. Write your own definition of wealth.

Chapter Six

Peruvian Proposal

Jim

Without a paddle

'The highest reward for a person's toil is not what they get for it but what they become by it.'
John Ruskin

I put my knife and fork together proclaiming: 'potatoes, potatoes more bloody potatoes.' Guide Daniel, proudly defended his country as he blew out cigarette smoke with a squint. 'What do you expect *amigo*? There are over 200 types of potato grown right here in Peru.' I thought about it and *we were* determined to eat like the locals so gave our *gracias* to the leathery-skinned waitress who took the remains of our *ceviche* (fish) away. If nothing else, there was no danger of us travelling to the jungle on an empty stomach.

"There are two ways to get us up to Lagunas," Daniel told us, suggesting we went into some shade to protect ourselves from the heat that was beating down.

"Does one of them involve an air-conditioned plane?" I asked, swatting away a persistent mosquito with my sheriff's hat.

"Afraid not," came the swift response. "Our option is a cramped 12-hour boat ride or the faster, more expensive four-hour "speed boat" trip."

For the price equivalent of a 20-minute bus ride into Chester, we spent the next few hours full-throttling up a tributary of the Amazon, dodging threatening pieces of driftwood. I was instructed to sit on a piece of plywood the size of a kid's swing seat and raise my arms when collision with driftwood was probable.

GO! Read

Around the world in 80 days, Michael Palin

White tourists were clearly a novelty in Lagunas and as we flopped out of the boat like refugees, we were swarmed by locals offering to take our bags or provide transport.

"Keep hold of your bags and keep close," Daniel warned, with constant *"Non, señors"* to insistent offers of help. *Gracias* but no thanks, the travellers were *his* guests.

I kept Emma close as we cradled our kit. One particularly grimy guy grabbed hold of Em's bag, possibly offering to help, but it was not a chance I was going to take. I had to take the bag, nudge him to one side and jostle aboard the waiting tuk-tuk. We sped off, leaving clouds of dust in our wake.

Emma

Lagunas turned out to be the largest jungle city in Peru with just over twelve thousand people, although life was very simple here and most of the people actually lived in the jungle, which surrounded the region that made up the city. There were no cars in Lagunas and only occasional streetlights flickering with insects and stray dogs. Our digs for the night were above an old excuse for a pharmacy, decked out with disturbingly dusty stock.

Jim

The backwater chemist was barely operational, with iron bars on the windows to keep out the locals and nets draped around the edge to deter the mozzies. Our host kindly gave us a tour of the dripping bathroom, washing line and our room. Candles flickered as we arrived; not to create a romantic ambience but because the lights went out in the whole town at midnight. Access to electricity was limited to only four hours a day.

"I know it's basic, but it's safe," assured Daniel as he slapped the back of his neck with a satisfying "Got him!"

"He has a disabled son who sits in on the shop floor," he continued. Daniel beckoned us to follow as we peered around the shop floor where, seated in an old rocking chair was Señor's disabled teenage son vacantly watching a distorted black and white TV blaring out an old Spanish cartoon. His miserable existence made us count our own blessings. But happiness, it seems, was relative. Señor's son seemed quite happy rocking away in his world, which consisted of a cold metal table, rough splintered floor, a couple of broken chairs and a dusty old black and white photograph of a man in military dress, oblivious to our presence. The facilities offered were a bucket of cold water in which to bathe.

GO! Think

There is a tribal grounding in going back to basics. What simple things in life do you yearn for?

Emma

Our lodgings were clean and at least provided my last few nights of sleeping in a real bed before having to rough it in the jungle. I planned to relish every moment. Just before lights out that first night, I heard a horrendous scream from downstairs. This was the start of our jungle experience.

The few days we spent in Lagunas were an education and gave us yet another insight to Peruvian life. Many of the people here in the city had been raised in the jungle, moving in only after getting married. Many of the shops looked like the front room of someone's house, doubling as the local bar or even a restaurant. One of them even served as the local cinema showing DVDs on one of the few TVs for miles around – but that was only if the generator was working. The houses were made of materials from the jungle, with open spaces for windows, dirt floors and animals that wandered in and out of any house they chose.

Jim

Emma, Daniel and I headed up the hot dusty trail to Manuel's, the local tour operator who worked from the front room of his wooden hut of a home. He'd built the place himself to house his nine kids, various pets and selection of rather scrawny looking 'main course' animals. His multi-tasking daughter, rustled up some fish, potato and bananas in a wok, with her baby under one arm and wok in the other. She only paused to breast-feed her daughter, in between chopping the onions.

Emma

Where have the red wellies gone?

'You gain strength, courage and confidence by every experience in which you really stop to look fear in the face. You must do the thing which you think you cannot do.'
Eleanor Roosevelt

Together with Manuel, Jim pored over a map for the rest of the afternoon, plotting our route to and around the Pacaya Samiria National Park, and talking about equipment. The locals call the park the 'mirror of the jungle' and it is regarded as one of the most important areas of biodiversity on the planet with hundreds of types of bird, fish and enough mammals, primates and amphibians to fill a zoo.

The only thing stopping Manuel and Jim from writing copious lists together was the language barrier. Jim thought he had found his second-in-command; or rather Manuel had found his second-in-command.

As boys were boys, I sat in the kitchen that was more like a log cabin with two large green parrots that had taken up residence in the rafters across the roof (note to self: in the presence of parrots, keep your hand over your cup of tea). To my amazement, I discovered that 16 people shared this humble house, which boasted only three main rooms.

That night, my concerns were raised following a conversation about tarantula nests and the fact that the creatures that reside in them, jump - very far - when they are scared. Thus far, I had survived without having any major spider incidents, but I was not too sure how the 'red welly' scenario would hold up when faced with the jumping variety. I had to secure everyone's promise that if they saw a spider, either on me or near me, that they would get me away from it before telling me its location. With this promise extracted, I could relax. That was, until evening came.

GO! Read
Feel the Fear and do it anyway, Susan Jeffers.

As I was cleaning my teeth, Daniel, who was at the next sink, started acting very strangely, putting his finger to his lips and beckoning for me to follow him. This was most unlike him, so I cautiously followed him, thinking there was a problem. Ten paces later, Daniel heaved a huge sigh of relief.

"Man, I never thought I would get you away! Thankfully you didn't see it."

"What are you on about Daniel, are you OK?" I replied, more than a little puzzled.

"There's a tarantula on the mirror, just behind the plant by your sink. I nearly ran for it myself, but couldn't leave you to face it alone."

Like someone poking at a toothache to try and make it better, what did I do? I cautiously approached the sink to see the spider for myself. Well, I don't think it's an understatement to say it's doubtful they make red wellies big enough to fit this spider. It was nearly the size of a cat. Daniel, I noticed, was keeping a safe distance, and remembering that they really could jump (statistically, this one would be capable of beating Jonathan Edwards in the triple jump) I beat a hasty retreat too. I was unsure of what to do next. I wasn't going near it, but neither could I leave it; I didn't want it returning in the morning at some inopportune moment. All Daniel and I could do was laugh helplessly.

Our tearful laughter brought out the owner of the pharmacy, who on seeing our predicament, was only too happy to help. She disappeared inside. I was expecting her to return with an amazing spider-catching contraption, or at the very least, a bowl big enough to trap the eight-legged offender. She did reappear very quickly, but rather than the spider trap I had anticipated, she came baring a feather duster. Apart from trying to tickle the thing to death, I couldn't see what she planned to do with it.

To my horror, that's exactly what she did: tickled it around the sink and up the mirror. My screams of abject horror convinced her she needed reinforcement. This arrived in the form of her sister, who came with yet another feather duster. Unbelievable.

Several minutes and lots of tickling later, Daniel finally leapt forward, jumping on the creature that had jumped on to the floor putting us all out of our misery.

Jim

When she related the story to me, the spider size had gone from the size of a cat, to that of a small dog. With Daniel not committing either way, choosing to shrug indifferently they admitted it may have been a bit smaller than they first thought. Fair play to Em though; a few months earlier she'd have passed out at the mere sight of even a money spider.

Emma

Up bright and early, packed and ready to leave for the jungle the next morning, I nipped to the loo for my last civilised visit for a while. Just as I had made contact with the toilet seat, it pounced: a spider, identical to the one from the previous night, which was climbing over the back of the toilet door.

To put you in the picture, the toilet cubicles were just about big enough to open the door without flattening you against the wall. The spider and I were trapped inside, both with growing panic. My screams brought Jim running, ready to fight off my attacker. The only problem was negotiating the logistics. Feeling helpless, Jim banged hard on the door, trying to open it. Of course, this only made matters worse as I could see the spider preparing to pounce. Asking Jim to retreat, I set about trying to release the bolt that now appeared to be glued into place. Every time I wiggled the lock, the spider crouched, ominously closer to jumping point.

What seemed like hours later, I managed to unbolt the door, flinging it open and making a vain attempt at freedom into Jim's waiting arms. It worked. I had lived through yet another spider encounter. Jim, curious to see what all the fuss was about, poked his head back round the door, only to retreat ashen faced.

"For once, Em, that is no exaggeration," he said. "*That* is the size of a goat."

What may have been a small insignificant act for many people, felt to me as if I had conquered Everest. That night I learnt that facing your fears is often not as bad as we imagine it will be. Still, two encounters in 24 hours and I was beginning to wonder just how bad it was going to get in the jungle.

Go! Think:
List 5 things that you fear, even on a small scale that would give you great satisfaction to conquer. What first steps can you take to begin conquering these fears.

Jim

Don't rock the boat

'Courage is ... when you stare your worst fear or toughest obstacle in the face and beat it.'
   Adam McCord

A two-hour journey on a local farmer's horse and cart saw our provisions and us delivered safely to the start of our jungle adventure.

Whistling I'm the King of the Swingers from *The Jungle Book*, we wobbled aboard and wedged ourselves in the middle of a hand-carved four-man canoe. I was finally about to put my Boy Scout days into practice. The closest I'd ever got to something similar was riding down the log flume at Alton Towers and being sick due to too many marshmallow snowballs. But the time had now come for us to survive on just our bare necessities.

GO! Read
If by Rudyard Kipling

One sneeze or cough in this canoe and we'd capsize. It was already floating precariously just two inches above the surface of the water, weighed down with all our belongings. Sonia, Manuel's wife, was our official cook who paddled from the rear as Manuel perched up in front, paddling on both sides of the boat. Em and I sat back on our rucksacks and enjoyed the unspoilt scenes around us. Daniel and a support guide were in a second, smaller, canoe complete with supplies and fishing nets. As I smothered my exposed legs with factor 40 I asked Daniel if there was anything we could do to help.

"No man, it's your holiday. Just sit back and enjoy," replied our chain-smoking guide. "Put plenty of that on man, you'll fry," squinted Daniel through smoke as he splashed river water over himself as his form of protection.

It was a searing, arid heat and within minutes I felt like jumping in the river. My skin was drying out rapidly and was beginning to resemble the bark of the canoe. Not a word was uttered as Manuel stoically rowed away, stopping and pointing out jungle life that we'd never otherwise have spotted. He would raise his hand to his ear and point to what appeared to be some random place in the trees. He knew the nooks and crannies of the riverbank and the places to drink as he supped handfuls of the muddy river water.

Tarantula nests the size of traffic cones frightened Emma out of her wits, but the mischievous monkeys made up for it. When two giant red ants joined us on the boat I was less welcoming. I rocked the boat madly in an attempt to get rid of them.

"Whoa! No chance!" called Daniel. Manuel will show you what to do. "That's just dangerous, man, you could fall into a crocodile's mouth by rocking the boat."

Manuel took over showing me the only way to get rid of these resilient critters by swiftly setting them alight. Oh, how they crackled.

Emma

Mozzie fodder

'Even mosquitos only get one chance.'
The Dalai Lama

Our campsites for the next few nights were clearings of land with access to the river. Our first site looked harmless enough with space for a 'his' and 'hers' bathroom, also known as a couple of trees, spaced far enough apart to afford some dignity.

Trees were one thing. What we were not prepared for were the mosquitoes. Our clothes covered every square inch of available flesh, and what was left exposed was plastered in repellent. But these things were ferocious. The flying hypodermics bit their way through not just one layer of clothing but several. Going to the loo was one of the biggest challenges we had faced so far as it meant exposing very sensitive areas of flesh, for what seemed to be very long periods of time. The dilemma was whether to hold off until desperation simply forced you to go, meaning going less often, but for longer periods of time or going as normal, which of course involved exposing flesh for shorter periods but with higher frequency. Either way, you knew that they were waiting for you the minute your trousers came down and it was really just a race against time.

Despite my efforts, I ended up with bites on parts of me that I never wish to repeat and quite frankly left me wondering at the audacity of the things. Eighty-seven bites. Counted by Jim's own fair hand as he administered the calamine lotion.

Jim

Jungle activity rose with the sun and the lighter it got the louder it became. Emma and I covered ourselves in more factor 40 and mozzie repellent and set off to enjoy the sights and sounds of the jungle by canoe. Manuel and Sonia skilfully manoeuvred us around, often only using one paddle and taking 'side-alley' short cuts. The sloths clinging to the side of the eucalyptus trees spent 23 hours of each day sound asleep and refused to stir despite Manuel's attempts at animal noises. Fishing nets that had been strategically laid the night before were retrieved to reveal a catch of piranha, stingray and a couple of prehistoric looking things with their shells still intact. I'd not normally be bothered what came out of tattered fishing nets but when your next meal depended on it there was more of a vested interest.

"If you step on one of those in the water, it injects its tail into you and that's you in hospital," explained Daniel as we inspected the flapping catch in the net.

"There's no hospital for miles, Dan the man," I retorted.

"Exactly. Why do you think I don't stand in the river?" he laughed.

Emma

By now, the luxuries of Dubai seemed a world away. The beauty of the jungle however was not quite enough to stop me wishing I was elsewhere. In truth, I would have gladly swapped the jungle experience to go back to our basic log cabin, which at this point, was looking like the height of luxury. But I was here now. And determined to make the most of it.

We ate like kings that week, however, on freshly caught fish from the nets that Manuel cast each evening before we went to bed. Despite the heat and relentless mosquitoes, we were in awe of the vastness and variety of the jungle and the noises changing with each hour that passed until a chorus of animal sounds reached its crescendo by dusk.

GO! Read
Herbs that heal, Michael A Weiner

The joy at our trip was soon cut short however. By the evening of day three, I woke with a nagging pain in my stomach. All was definitely not well. My pain quickly turned to agony. Waking Jim up to send the advance party to the 'bathroom' to check for webs, I flew past him before he even got the chance, unable to hold on. The mad dash was then repeated every five minutes for the next hour until the others started to wake. I realised that unless there was a rapid improvement, there was no way I could spend the following day in a canoe. With severe stomach cramps, a desperate need for the bathroom, and a fever that was rising by the minute, I was miserable.

We informed Manuel of my state of health. He disappeared into the jungle with a knowing smile, returning after half an hour.

"Hjeer, dreenk dis, muy beuno," he said, holding out what can only be described as a steaming potion straight from the set of *Harry Potter*. "No, no, I'll be OK, honestly," I protested as I made a swift exit for the nearest clearing out of range.

GO! Think:
What alternative methods have you considered to heal yourself of ills?

I returned a little sheepishly, took the potion from his grasp, sniffed it, checked for floating eyeballs and, under the watchful stare of the whole group, drank it on the promise of instant improvement. Surprisingly, within an hour, I felt confident enough to get back into the canoe. But it was decided, in light of my afflictions, that we would head back to civilisation. As we wearily disembarked from our vessel, hot, saturated and cramped, a royal blue butterfly looped around the canoe, settling on a clump of reeds as though it were seeing the walking wounded on their way.

Jim
A wider perspective on the slow boat to Iquitos.

'We judge others by their behaviour. We judge ourselves by our intentions'
Ian Percy

We left Lagunas early the following day for a 36-hour river 'cruise' to the city of Iquitos. Our transportation was a large, rusty, tin boat, for which we had purchased tickets and hammocks. The floating wreck arrived at four in the morning while the mist still hung over the river, giving it the eerie look of a ghost ship coming to take its cargo of unfortunate souls up river. We piled on board, together with a large buffalo, two white oxen, a crate of chickens, a dozen young pigs, miles of steel cables, a few hundred boxes of salt and a small mountain of green bananas. Our floating prison, with cold steel window bars, filthy floor and pots of gruel-like soup made me feel like I was part of a social experiment. As I tried out various unstable ways to lie and read a philosophy book in a hammock, a gaunt looking woman carrying a child in a bright orange papoose boarded just as we were about to leave and float off into the dark Amazonian night. She had no hammock and I busied myself reading as I simply couldn't find it within me to offer her my place.

GO! Read
Status Anxiety, Alain De Botton

We guarded our kits as we stuck out like sore thumbs on this boat. No such vigilance from Daniel and Emma, who were fast asleep. As I reached over to grab Emma's Sony Cyber-shot to get a photo of her with her mouth wide open, there was an almighty CRACK just as I got my hands on the camera. It sounded as though the boat had been ripped in two.

"What, what's going on?" asked a dazed Emma.

"Lightening," I replied. We'd gone headlong into a tropical storm. "You won't need the flash to photograph this. Just look at it."

The thunder and lightning were enough to stir even Daniel from his hammock. Water gushed into one end of the vessel as we witnessed the brightest of white lights illuminating the whole boat, the river and jungle outside. With each flicker of light, passengers left their hammocks to don all their belongings to save them getting wet. I valued my life more and despite having faith in my rubber-soled flip flops insisted that we stay in our hammocks to watch the electric storm. All the blood drained from Emma's face. Wide-eyed she empathised with the caged animals, who were desperate to escape and quietly resigned herself to staying in her hammock. Once the hellish storm had passed we settled back down.

Emma

Relieved to have survived the previous night's storm I went out on deck to get some fresh air, leaving the boys to guard the bags. It was a fascinating scene watching the sun rise as we relentlessly chugged on. The delivery of cargo to the various villages on the way, from a box of canned milk to a large reel of cable. The instant our boat touched the riverbank, the boxes, cartons or spools of whatever goods were being delivered were unceremoniously dumped on the ground before the boat-hands pushed off again to continue the journey. The boat was obviously the main lifeline to the outside world for those who lived here.

During one of my 'fresh air' breaks, I heard a loud siren blaring somewhere behind us.

I assumed the boat was sounding its horn to warn traffic upstream of our approach, but the siren got louder and more frequent until I realised it was a river police craft in hot pursuit of us. At least six uniformed men waved their arms and gestured for us to stop. Being the only foreigners on board, I had visions of us being their target, and carted off having committed some unanticipated offence only to be lost in Peru forever without a trace.

I braced myself for a sudden stop as our boat headed straight for the bank. Jim and Daniel were fast asleep 'guarding' the bags, oblivious to the whole episode. As we reached the riverbank, a very tall thin man and a young boy hurried past me carrying a large, red plastic dustbin. They then leapt to solid ground and ran for cover towards the trees. As they did so, all six policemen boarded, causing a huge commotion among the passengers. Looking back to the trees, I saw that the bin and its bearers had disappeared into the thickets. We pulled away from the bank promptly, leaving the two castaways stranded in what appeared to be the middle of nowhere.

Looking around to see if anyone else had witnessed this bizarre scene, I appeared to have been alone. The captain now had his arm around the most officious-looking policeman and was reassuring him that no-one of any interest to them was on board. He then handed the cops three huge bagfuls of food, a bribe, I guessed, to smooth over the situation.

I had picked up enough Spanish to understand the gist of the conversation, but was too stunned to do anything about it. They were searching for a fugitive whom they believed was travelling with a small boy. I desperately hoped that they wouldn't start to question everyone on board as I am not sure I wanted to get involved in anything underhand. To my relief the police took the food, got back into their boat and sped off, leaving me with a few nagging questions. If I had been able to speak fluent Spanish would I have said anything? After all, I had seen the fugitives make their getaway. If this had happened in the UK would I have come forward? And if I had done so, would I have been helping or interfering? Without all the facts there can often be a fine line between the two. I concluded that in this situation it was best to let sleeping dogs lie. But that didn't quieten my mind of the guilt of not sharing what I had seen.

When I returned to the hammocks, I expected to see Jim and Daniel excitedly dissecting the incident, but instead I was met with two snoring, open-mouthed sloths, who had slept through the whole thing.

GO! Think:
Looking at something from a different perspective; it may help you see different possibilities. What are the possibilities?

Curbing enthusiasm

'You will never stub your toe standing still.'
Charles Kettering

Back in civilisation once more, we basked in the luxury of a hot shower, a soft bed, a hearty lunch and clean laundry. Jim even indulged in some of the lavender shower gel that he previously scoffed at.

Jim
As needs must, Emma and Daniel explored the shops, leaving me

to my own devices to plan my pending proposal in the South. Aside from catching up with reality, Google would help me decide exactly where in the lost city of Machu Picchu I would propose. The ancient civilization may not approve of rituals such as proposals and I wanted to be clear, (or as clear as I could be through a search engine) that the spot I picked wasn't meant for some sacrificial lama.

I learned that an explorer called Hirham Bingham had discovered Machu Picchu some 400 years after it had been mysteriously abandoned by the Incas in the fifteenth century and 'reclaimed by the jungle'. It escaped detection for several centuries until local farmers led an American explorer to the site in 1911, who went on to uncover part of its once-secret glory.

Apparently, Spanish conquistadors made no record of this mystical place when they rode into town 500 years ago. Part of the sacred site, Huayna Picchu, meaning 'young mountain', was reputed to look majestically over the lush terraces of the lost city with a climb to its summit that wasn't for the faint-hearted. It was the fascinating background of all this ancient history that suggested to me that standing on the top of the world might be the ideal place for asking Em to grow old with me.

Everything was falling into place and my to-do e-list was practically complete until an email from my friend Paul, who had organised a charity trek to Machu Picchu arrived. His note was not what I'd expected. He reported that two nights previously the people he had been trekking with had been attacked on the Inca Trail. The eight-strong group with over twenty guides, whilst asleep had been set upon, mugged and bound. Although they had guides with them they were no match for the muggers who pistol-whipped them, broke a couple of their fingers and threatened to shoot anyone who resisted giving up their belongings.

Emma

While I left Jim behind and was out busying myself with shopping, I was too busy dodging the tuk-tuks while crossing the road to notice a raised man-hole cover. As I accidentally kicked it, I heard a loud crack followed by an overwhelming pain.

Looking down at my foot expecting to see pools of blood, I was at first surprised to see it looking perfectly normal, without so much as a scratch. That was until, several minutes later, my toe had turned a rich shade of purple, was double its normal size and was screaming to be free of my shoe. It was excruciating. The awful thought of having to cancel the Inca Trail – the main purpose for our trip to Peru – suddenly shot into my mind.

The Inca Trail had always been Jim's goal and I knew how important it was to him. I was determined not to let him down and, swearing Daniel to secrecy, I decided to try to play down how serious it was, hobbling back to the internet café to collect Jim.

Jim

As I re-read Paul's message in disbelief, in limped an unusually down-trodden Emma. I had to chuckle at her dilemma considering we had escaped virtually unharmed from the jungle – apart from an upset stomach that still persisted.

"Come on, we need to get you fit for the biggie. Let's have a look at that toe. You've got to be fit to conquer the lost civilization," I tried to reassure her.

"It's not life threatening, Jim. You seem a bit out of sorts yourself. What's wrong?" Secrets weren't my strong point and it was only fair that she knew. "I've had some bad news from Paul."

This could potentially shatter my dream of a romantic proposal and at this stage all we could do was send our commiserations to Paul and the group, count our blessings and wait for more information. Daniel was as shocked as we were at the news and had never heard of anything like it happening on the trail before. It made national and international news. A manhunt was on as the local authorities took a threat to their main source of tourist dollars very seriously.

Emma took another turn for the worse. Feeling ill, coupled with her throbbing toe she retired to bed leaving Daniel and I alone. He enlightened me on what had really happened to Paul and the charity group. Six months earlier the police had been told they were no longer required to man the Inca Trail as it was perfectly safe. Arrests had already been made and police-issue guns had been rounded up. The police were now only paid to stamp passports and take money from paying tourists. The authorities decided to pull the plug as their presence was thought to be unnecessary on a peaceful trail.

While Emma was ill in bed for the next couple of days, still suffering from an upset stomach, Daniel and I marked time in the city hoping that she would recover for the key part of our journey. I used the time to finalise not only the proposal but also our Thai beach wedding, spa and honeymoon. Poor Emma lay there in the half dark in a sorry state. She was dehydrated, light-headed and felt sick.

Rejecting my offering of Lucozade, grapes and chocolate, sleepy Emma was definitely not herself. Facing another flight, I quietly packed for us both preparing to fly south. But watching Emma lying there made me doubt the likelihood of the Inca Trail happening - and what about my proposal? Daniel bade us farewell. Half our Peru trip was now over and he wouldn't be accompanying us on our alleged tourist-friendly southern leg.

"Hey guys, good news!" he said, slapping me on the shoulder like an old friend. "The police are back on the Inca Trail. All you need to do is get better! Please take it easy."

"We'll be fine," croaked Em as I darted to the nearest lavatory. Now it was my turn to be ill.

GO! Think:

Your true self – what situations help you recognise or identify your true self?

Emma

Great expectations and eternal hope

'If you're going through hell … keep going.'
   Winston Churchill

After feeling like the only tourists in town when we had been in the north, it was strange to see other people with cameras around their necks wandering the streets. Here we were not the gringos that were greeted with a friendly smile, but the rich, Western tourists who could line the natives' pockets with money. Our hotel in Arequipa, had a garden filled with lush greenery, deep pink bougainvillea covering the walls and birdsong that filled the air from dawn until dusk. Still not having recovered from my stomach upset, all I could manage was to crawl into bed with a cursory grunt and stay there for the rest of the afternoon and evening, leaving Jim to fend for himself again.

My nausea and stomach cramps were now coming in waves rather than the constant pain I had been experiencing earlier, which made me believe I was getting better. We had a two-day trip planned to the Colca Canyon to see the condors, the most part of which was to be spent on a bus. Not ideal for someone with a problem like mine. The buses in the north had been amazing; the seats reclined, food was served and, importantly, there was a toilet on board. If that was in the north where the tourists didn't go, how much better would the buses in the south be where tourism was the mainstay of the economy? I was confident. Waiting patiently on the pavement for our super, deluxe bus to collect us we ignored the rattling minibus that stopped in front of us. Where were the reclining seats, the food and most importantly the toilet? Oh no.

We spent two days on the bone-shaker that would take us in search of the condors at Colca Canyon, only to be told when we arrived that it was in fact the mating season and it was unlikely that any birds would be seen. True to the guide's word, there was not a condor in sight. And who could blame them. What would you do given a choice between performing for a bus-load of tourists or mating?

Jim

I didn't see any improvement in Em's condition. Despite attempting to re-hydrate, sucking on coca sweets, chewing on leaves and adding iodine to everything we drank, Emma was clearly in need of medical attention. She was deteriorating and had lost her usual healthy glow. I was weak and achy but could still walk unaided. A flash of pushing her up the 3,000 steps of the Inca Trail in a wheelchair came and went. I stared out to the dry white cliffs of our barren surroundings. Emma clutched one of her many crystals, this time tourmaline, a black coal like rock that is allegedly 'very powerful'. She weakly held my hand and reminded me that 'the angels would decide' if we were to do the trail or not.

Emma

Doctor's Orders

'Nothing can bring you peace but yourself.'
Ralph Waldo Emerson

All I wanted to do was to get back to Arequipa, collect our bags and get to Cuzco, where we had four days to get ready for the 'big trip'. Surely, I would have recovered by then. Jim however, was now adamant that we call a doctor. I was beginning to agree with him. I had reached the conclusion that, in this state, I could not physically do the Inca Trail. Something had to be done, but it would have to wait until we reached Cuzco. The only saving grace of taking things easy was that I didn't have to walk very far because my toe, still purple and swollen, was not up to much more than a gentle stroll.We arrived at Cuzco, which, we learnt meant the 'earth's navel' and was the birthplace of the Inca empire. How apt. We sat there with weak tummies, splitting headaches and dry skin, wishing we could take our minds off our navel areas for once. Taking our passports back from the receptionist tears welled up in my eyes as I finally admitted to Jim that I was really ill. Jim insisted that he call a doctor immediately. I could barely stand by this time and collapsed into a weeping mess on one of the chairs in reception.

Thankfully an English-speaking doctor came to the rescue.

"'ospital for you, Señorita," he declared.

I was horrified and in my stubbornness flatly refused – after all, I only had an upset stomach. After taking my blood pressure three times, because he thought his equipment was broken, I was told that with a reading of 75 over 55, I shouldn't even be able to stand. Much to Jim's horror I reached a deal with the doctor; if I promised to stay in bed for at least 48 hours and drink copious amounts of electrolyte, he would not insist on taking me to hospital. As he was about to leave, Jim miraculously developed the same symptoms as me and asked to be examined.

The doctor listened patiently, finally handing him some pills so he wouldn't feel left out, and said that if there was no improvement in me in the next eight days, he would not take no for an answer and would send me straight to hospital.

Whether Jim was actually sick, or whether he just came out in sympathy for me I will never know, but within two hours he was in bed shivering as though he were in the Arctic.

GO! Think
What is the difference between determination and stubbornness?

Jim
"This is our dress rehearsal for the mountain," I joked, slowly putting on my second fleece, woolly hat and thick socks, as I weakly dragged myself into bed next to Emma, who was red hot.
"I'm still freezing," she shivered.
"Me too."

Emma
Jim's 'critical illness' cleared up by the next day. He was up and around by the morning and left me sleeping in bed.

Jim
Wandering around the colourful main square, the Plazade de Aramis, was hard work on an empty belly at altitude and proved to be a great effort. A demonstration of placard-bearing locals had started. Riot police were on standby and they were blocking the hordes of protestors from entering the town hall. A British couple told me it was a protest over poor pay, high taxes and the low standard of living in the region.

Over a coffee in a local café I watched the crowds gather and the atmosphere cool in time with my steaming hot latté. A breathless mooch around some handicraft shops made me a target for local orphans who wanted to sell me postcards, polish my open-toed sandals (brave) and sell me a cigarette lighter. This once-thriving place was now counting on the hordes of people intent on visiting Machu Picchu.

A proposal meant an engagement ring and amongst the countless alpaca smocks, hats and silver spoons were display counters full of locally-made jewellery. Then I spotted a silver ring adorned with three Inca crosses (red, green and blue). It fitted on my little finger, which, I figured, would equate to Em's ring finger, and I bought it without a second thought. This would accompany me along the Inca Trail, hopefully with a fully-recovered potential fiancée by my side. Something about that ring had grabbed me.

Emma

On his return, Jim brought all sorts of tempting information about shops and restaurants he had discovered and the spa that was attached to the hotel. Tempted as I was, if I didn't stay in bed and recover now, then the Inca Trail would be forgotten. After all, the bed rest had given my toe time to heal and it was now returning to its normal colour. Jim reassured me that we would get to Machu Picchu somehow, even if we were bussed in like many of the tourists. But I hadn't come this far to be taken there by bus.

So, for once, I was a good patient and followed doctor's orders. Our new guide for the seven-day trek came to the hotel to brief us about our week's camping trek. He took one look at me and had serious doubts that I would make the first day, let alone the 5,000 metre climb over Salcantay Mountain.

"You are white like flour and I don't think it is just your English skin," commented Juan.

"I just need a little fresh air to get some colour in my cheeks, I'll be fine," I answered, not quite sure who I was trying to convince the most - me or him. There were still 36 hours to recover my strength. I would be fine.

Twelve hours later, the doctor returned and was satisfied enough with my recovery not to ship me off to the hospital. Another 36 hours later, we were standing on the pavement outside our hotel ready for the seven-day trek that would finally take us to Machu Picchu. This was the reason for coming to South America. With the right amount of determination, a little dreaming, some stubbornness and a lot of hope, it is amazing what you can achieve.

GO! Think:
What is your next goal?
How determined are you to achieve it?

Much to my relief the first three days were to be spent on horseback. Although I was feeling much better, I was not quite ready for walking eight hours a day at altitude.

Jim

Climb every mountain

'There is nothing that makes its way more directly into the soul than beauty.'
    Joseph Addison

The remote village of Molla Poto was the start of our Inca Trail. Juan introduced us to the expedition team: a chef, support chef, two porters, three horses and a couple of mules that were laid on for us. All we had to do was stay on our horses, take the altitude and arrive at base camp on the Inca Trail. Bags were packed, wrapped in the customary blue tarpaulin, buckles fastened and stirrups adjusted. Patting my steed, I announced that I was to refer to him as Dobbin for the duration.

"What's yours called?" I asked Emma.

"Patch," she replied, feeding her horse an apple.

The porters worked quickly, were fit and strong and didn't need anything I'd brought on the kit list. Hiking boots, essential for our warmth and protection, were way above their needs. Their footwear was limited to a pair of old trainers or open-toed sandals.

Emma

We rode gently through fields and tracks, slowly making our way up into the mountains, with snow-covered peaks as a backdrop. The weather was kind to us. The sun shone on our backs and a gentle breeze blew in our faces. At lunchtime, we let the horses graze and were asked to sit back and rest by our guides, not being allowed to lift a finger to help. With so much rustling and clanking coming from behind the bushes, we assumed they were finding the food to prepare a small picnic.

Ten minutes later, out came a table, tablecloth, chairs, cutlery, china and salt and pepper. This was my kind of camping. Could it get any better?

Yes, it could.

Soup served with warm, freshly prepared garlic bread was followed by *al dente* spaghetti and a delicately flavoured fresh tomato sauce, rounded off with china cups of proper tea and McVitie's chocolate biscuits. Jim and I were flabbergasted that such a feast was not only rustled up so quickly but that we were sitting at tables and chairs being waited on in the middle of a camping trip in the remote Andean mountains.

Jim

Having realised that we knew little about the significance of the sacred origins of the area, Juan explained how mountains, lakes, boulders and caves are believed to possess supernatural powers and are timeless representations of supernatural beings. I noticed that Juan was wearing a Southern Cross talisman around his neck, similar in shape to the ring I'd stashed safely away in my backpack. Emma rode on leaving the dense plant life behind her for open scrub. I hung back and asked Juan the significance of this hand-crafted alabaster cross.

"It's from the Sacred Valley of the Incas," he said as he pointed over to snow-capped Salcantay whose brown lower slopes dominated the vista. He explained that the real Southern Cross is the primary guiding constellation of the South American night sky and is represented in all shamanic ceremonies that invoke sacred space. The special cross on a string he wore carried the rich spiritual symbolism of the Andean mountain people and allowed man to get to know himself.

"So this means a lot to your people?" I asked, tightening the reins on my stubborn horse who had decided it was time for some grass eating.

"Of course, this is everything. It brings all the opposites together, like you and Emma, male and female."

What a coincidence. The ring I'd bought, purely on its aesthetic attraction, represented the Southern Cross and symbolised the three tiers of Inca life: the lower world, this world and the higher world. The three levels are also represented by the snake, the puma and the condor. With visions of Emma on top of Salacanty Pass being laid out naked as we danced circles around her I realised how serious Juan took his history. He interrupted my sick fantasy as he pointed out some ominous-looking grey clouds that were gathering over his symbolic mountain as we reached the end of the foothills.

Our idyllic dream was interrupted with a torrential downpour just as we were at our most exposed Our guides threw up our tent and the lean-to kitchen in minutes as the rain and darkness rapidly descended.

We needed to get warm and there was no firewood. Despite layers of shirts, a couple of pairs of socks, hats and fleeces we were still cold. My appetite was non-existent at 4,000 metres. I tried to take on board some potato and soup but could only manage a mugful of coca leaf tea. I battled against my rapid pulse, hangover-like headache and breathlessness. Em carried on regardless.

Amongst the blanket of glistening stars we spotted the Southern Cross in the sky and a single shooting star. My wish was that we would make it safely to the top and that my achy neck could recover from stargazing.

Emma
Calamity Jim - one man and his horse

'The greatest glory never comes from falling, but from rising each time you fall.'
Clay Aiken

As we woke in the morning, looking forward to another day in the saddle, we eagerly climbed out of the tent to be hit with a view that will stay with me forever. Salcantaye Mountain had been covered in cloud and creeping darkness when we arrived the night before but now stood there at the head of a gentle valley, with the sun reflecting off its snow-covered peak. Things just kept getting better.

Jim

Dobbin took some coercing that morning and I learned, when required, how to whip his backside. I only felt partly in control and had to put my faith in my four-legged friend. One slip and there would be no star-gazing that night.

"Are you alright, Jim?" asked Em as she heard me talking to my horse.

"It's not responding, bloody thing."

"Patience, Babe, we're at altitude ..."

"Don't tell me, I'm flogging a dead horse ..." I cried back, hauling the reins, clucking and kicking in a desperate attempt to get Dobbin moving.

As we wound around a perilously high ridge it was time for a bucking bronco experience.

Emma

The first I heard of the trouble was an accusatory 'Emma' shouted out from behind me as though I had done something to the horse. Looking back, I saw an uncertain Jim holding on for dear life but the horse appeared to be completely calm so I was a little puzzled as to what the problem was.

"Don't laugh, my horse has turned into a bucking bronco, I don't think he liked getting his hooves wet in that stream," protested Jim as I quietly chuckled to myself.

"Well, if Buckaroo starts again, sit up tall and try and keep his head up. Otherwise, just make sure you land on your feet when you come unstuck," I replied, trying to be constructive.

Just as we started climbing the foothills of the mountain came another more urgent scream of "Emma!" As I looked round, Buckaroo lived up to his name, sending Jim hurtling backwards over the horse's rump soon to be accompanied by the saddle and blankets. Jim landed very cleverly on his feet (obviously taking heed at my advice) with the saddle between his legs and looking rather shell-shocked. The horse having shed its load was now contentedly grazing at the side of the track without a care in the world.

GO! Read

The horse whisperer by Nicholas Evans

Jim

I was expecting the guides to hold up score cards out of 10 for my technique. Emma, upon realising I was OK, proceeded to collapse laughing and for a change, the guides followed. I didn't quite know what to do next except to take it and laugh.

"Dobbin will be dog food if he bloody tries that again," I added, brushing myself down. "I nearly had a coronary."

"It's better than walking," replied Emma.

I was annoyed, embarrassed and lucky to be still standing. "No it's not, clearly not. I'm walking the thing up. I'll take this mountain on," I grimaced.

The strap under Dobbin's belly had slipped back, repeatedly trapping what was left of his male bits, giving him every reason to buck like he did. After a few steps I was breathless so I stood back and watched the horses and guides carry on as if they were out on a Sunday morning stroll.

Emma

Getting to the top of the pass at 5,000 metres above sea level felt like an incredible achievement especially when I thought about how ill I had been the week before.

As we neared the start of the tourist part of the Inca Trail, we went through valleys with more and more signs of life. The wide valleys showed signs of the Inca civilization all around us. Terraces groaning with a variety of crops and scattered rocks showed where the ancient houses had once stood. Cattle and sheep littered the hillsides and our cook went off to one of the farms to buy a chicken for dinner that night.

We were soon meeting other groups of horses, loaded with building materials heading back up the valley from where we had come, closely followed by the farmers who had trekked for a day to go and get the materials to build their houses. We were in the midst of an equine rush hour. Our camping in the solitude of the wilderness was over as we approached the first of our official 'Inca' campsites. Still, there was one benefit of commercialisation: proper lavatories and basins.

Jim

In the footsteps of the Incas

'We are not human beings on a spiritual journey. We are spiritual beings on a human journey.'
Pierre Teillhard de Chardin

"Mother Earth, or *Pachamama*, was kind, let us pass, no problem.

We have given back to her and we have luck on our side," grinned Juan, splashing his face in the river of Andean glacial melted snow.

It must have been freezing. Seeing as this was a public campsite other pre-Inca groups were pitched up alongside us with their entourage of porters, guides and supplies. This was as far as our horses would be taking us. It was to be on foot from here on.

Emma

My strength had returned over the last few days on horseback and now was the time for the real workout. Each step of the trail, worn down by many thousands of footsteps over the centuries, had been carved by hand and carefully placed to create a pathway to a sacred site. It was hard work. Jim showed incredible patience. Without him, I would not have had either the strength or the motivation to carry on in some places.

However testing, the trail was stunningly beautiful. Rain forests, hidden lakes and Inca ruins revealed through the clouds only added to our mounting excitement at reaching our desti-nation. After we had passed through a stone archway a stairway appeared from nowhere with over-hanging creepers and a carpet of moss on the parts of the stone not worn over time by tramping feet. I half expected to see Prince Charming leaping up the stairs, two by two, in his quest for Sleeping Beauty. Instead, my own Prince Charming was steadily making his way down the stairs behind me.

Jim

Upon approaching the 4,200 metre peak of Dead Woman's Pass (*Warmiwanusca*) we encountered clusters of other tourists keen to add the Machu Picchu badge to their rucksacks.

"Dead woman's pass, the highest point on the Inca trail, love" I announced.

"Charming, I haven't even walked over it yet and you're writing me off," Emma replied, smiling at a couple of breathless trekkers.

"They call it that because the rock formations resemble a woman lying on her back." I added.

"Keep it clean," came the reply.

Stopping for an apple break we descended into Inca territory, looking back at the ant-like trails of trekkers around us and failing to see anything resembling a dead woman.

We passed several ruins that allowed us to rest and enjoy the spectacular views of the nearby mountain ranges. Walking on an incredibly well-preserved stone Inca pathway we passed more ruins with plenty of time for an in-depth tour from Juan before entering a tunnel and a spiral staircase. It was amazing to think that nature had carved this and man had just adapted the stone without any disruption. Juan pointed out the many species of orchids, multicoloured birds on the dreamlike landscapes. It felt great to be on this path, the two of us together.

Emma

I had read many articles describing the Inca Trail as this spiritual journey. The first day I was expecting to hear voices from heaven telling me I was on the right path and was a little disappointed when this did not happen. When I had time to reflect on this (and believe me, climbing up these steps you have plenty of time to think), it became clear to me that it was all about taking what you can from the journey. As we progressed I became conscious of the pure history of the Trail.

GO! Think
What Path are you on? Where is it taking you?

Jim
As we trekked onwards and dusk fell, up and down the slippery

slopes of the end of our 35 mile Inca Trail it was looking increasingly as if we'd make it at least to the sun gate, the sacred entrance of the equinox. The whole experience began to feel like a civil engineer's nightmare as we crossed dense forests, deep canyons, and archaeological sites. All the irrigation canals, agricultural terracing, walls and shrines were proof of how ahead of their time these people were. It proved just how much these people worked with nature to prove that definition of civil engineering as 'harnessing nature for the benefit of mankind'.

With the high peaks now behind us we started our final day with a 4am hike down into the Cloud. Several breathless hefty climbs up stairs later we finally caught our first glimpse of the historic Forest on a magical winding Inca stairway to the place they call Winay Wayna, meaning forever young in the local lingo of Quechua. Another discreet delve into my backpack confirmed the ring was still in place, hopefully soon to be on Em's finger, as I trekked nervously on towards the sanctuary of Machu Picchu, even tipping Juan off about my intentions and sharing my plans of why and how with him.

Emma

On the last night of the trek, before we reached our final destination, I barely slept. We had gone through so much in the last six weeks from the north to the south of Peru, it was hard to believe that in the next few hours we would be at our personal summit of the trip. It had been our goal for so long that I was now very nervous in case it didn't meet our expectations. I concluded that regardless of what we thought about it, it was the journey to get there that had taught us so many things along the way.

GO! Think

When have you ever focused so hard on a goal that you forgot to enjoy the journey along the way?

Hit the peak

'To visit Machu Picchu you must prepare the soul, sharpen the senses. Forget for some minutes, the small and transcendental problems of our lives, of modern man.'

Napoleon Polo

I think we both must have felt the same about the depth of our feelings for what we were experiencing. We both ate our breakfast in almost silence, yet our expressions were serene. Once fed, Jim became even more energetic than usual and was eager to get going.

Jim

I was amongst the walls and buildings of the most enchanting place I had ever visited. This was far more than just crossing it off my list of places to see before I died. The excruciating hike on the trail, following in the footsteps of past pilgrims had built up to make everything more magical. The terraces were so imposing, stacked there like a giant's deck of cards and provided incredible views through the morning mist. As the sun heated the landscape around me, fronds of thin cloud rose to reveal the wonder of Machu Picchu for once leaving me utterly lost for words.

It was remarkably quiet and lacked the hordes of tourists we'd expected. Word got around that there was no train service running to this site today. There was a miners' strike that had resulted in the tracks being blocked leaving three throngs of tourists with no route up to the citadel. We were two of just 200 people that day to visit the lost city: ten per cent of the usual number.

This was huge, far bigger than I had imagined. It was all related to astronomy, universal consciousness and planning so ahead of its time that it made me wonder what technology they had at their disposal.

Despite Juan's knowledge of this sacred place with its dizzying vertical terraces, old temples, symbolic stairs and rocks I had even bigger things on my mind. The day of the proposal had arrived.

Emma

On the way through the ruins Juan, our guide, tried to explain about certain buildings and their significance, pointing out specific features that had been discovered over the years. But Jim did not seem interested and was really not listening. I couldn't understand it. Then he pointed to the small mountain that overlooked the whole of Machu Picchu.

Jim

As Juan enthusiastically dispensed his wisdom, it was becoming clear to him that I had my thoughts elsewhere when he asked: "Watt izz ze problem, Jheem?"

"I'd like to move on and climb Huyanu Picchu." I pointed to the objective of my mission. "Do you mind if we stop talking and save our energy so we can reach the top before lunch?"

"But this is interesting, Jim, he's sharing history with us," added Emma who was quite prepared to let him finish his spiel.

I gazed at Juan and directed my eyes over to where I wanted to be.

"OK, now we move on. Huyanu closes in a couple of hours."

"Closes? What do you mean, closes?" I asked with disbelief.

Emma

Unbelievable – we had trekked, climbed camped and conquered in the last seven days. We had reached our goal, and yet Jim was not taking the time to enjoy it. All Mr Action Man could think about was climbing more mountains.

Jim

The last climb was at 13:00 hrs to ensure the tourists who braved the climb were down at a reasonable time. There was a reason for this and it was not hard to see why. Our almost vertical scramble was breathtaking in many ways as I admired Em's tenacity in climbing up the ropes and ladders and scaling the rocks, sometimes on her hands and knees. I felt very little breathlessness as adrenaline took over when we reached the summit with a knowing handshake from Juan as I decided it was time to choose my moment to propose to the girl with whom I wanted to spend the rest of my life. She'd made it! I patiently waited for a couple of German hikers to remove themselves from what appeared to be the best vantage point. A pinnacle of rock that could comfortably accommodate two weary travellers overlooking the ancient city.

Emma

After conquering what I hoped would be my last difficult climb of the day, I collapsed on to one of the rocks to enjoy the view. Jim however, still would not settle. Within minutes, he was off, scrabbling over rocks to get the best vantage point on an outcrop of rock that appeared to hang in mid air. My heart was in my mouth as Jim climbed across ledges and gaps in the rocks – one slip and it would all be over. I could not look.

Go! Read

Summit Strategies, Secret to Mastering the Everest in you Life, Gary Scott and Dick Bass

Jim

"Would you mind if I sat there after you, guys, there's something I really need to do?"

They both shuffled off the rock and headed down towards a less ominous position. It was meant to be, call it angels, crystals or serendipity, I had the perfect spot. All I needed now was Emma.

Emma

Disbelief did not quite cover what I felt when Jim insisted that I join him on the outcrop of rock! He would not take no for an answer. So in what looked like the second instalment of Indiana Jones, I followed his footsteps, shutting my mind to the 300 metre drop and praying that my shaking knees would hold up.

Jim

As I nervously peeled an orange and drank more water, I watched toy-like excavators clearing the jungle from some newly discovered ruins far below. The ring was now safely in my pocket waiting for the right moment.

I imagined Incas walking around those ruins and tried to keep calm and focus on the job in hand. Orange, then propose. Orange, then propose. Emma finally edged her way over to me and with a little helping hand she was beside me on the ledge.

My heart was pounding so fast now, I was sure she would notice ...

"Isn't this just stunning?" she asked as she finally stood next to me on the rock. "OK, I admit it was worth the climb."

What had this place been like when it was at its full glory? It seemed hard to imagine a better place to pop the question. Pulling her towards me I took a deep breath and smiled.

"Emma, will you marry me?"

Emma

My stomach did a double back flip and tied itself in a double knot. My knees, still shaking from the shock of the climb, nearly gave way but I didn't need any time to consider my answer. It really was worth the climb!

"Yes. Yes I will. I'd love to. It would be an honour," I said, looking down as Jim placed a beautiful silver ring, decorated with three coloured symbols, on the third finger of my left hand. It was gorgeous. What was more, it fitted!

"Thank God for that!"

"What?"

"I mean, phew! I mean hurray, oh bloody hell, thanks, Emma."

And he took me in his strong, sun-tanned arms and hugged me so tightly I could hardly breathe. Then, fortunately, he relaxed his hold and kissed me, just like they do on the movies. And we stayed there holding each other for what felt like forever until Jim pulled away, and we stood, side by side with our arms around each other, staring down at the view, which defied all words, and feeling silent, at peace and at one with the past, the present and our future together.

Jim's restlessness over the past few hours now made sense.

"Um, Emma, by the way, I planned our wedding. I hoped so much that you would say yes!"

"What? More surprises?" Despite a stomach full of butterflies and my heart in my mouth I found I was grinning from ear to ear.

"What do you think all the internet sessions were for?" asked Jim, laughing with relief. He was amazed that I had not guessed.

Hand in hand, our minds now buzzing with excitement and preparations, we sat and finally drank in the magical atmosphere of where we were.

Jim

After all these months of planning and what seemed like an eternity keeping my intentions to myself feelings of utter joy and relief hit me hard. Sharing my future with a kindred spirit was everything I'd hoped for. I was a lucky man.

The location, the weather, the lack of tourists and the fact I'd shifted two territorial Germans off the best seat in the house all pointed to fate playing a hand. Nothing was going to stop me proposing on that rock right there and then, it was our place, our moment. Call it angels, crystals or ley lines but that day the universe conspired to help us and it all came together beautifully.

Go! Think
How do you celebrate achieving a goal?

Emma
Finally, after descending the mountain in half the time of the ascent, we returned to nearby civilization to celebrate. We were already so excited by our future together, but the bigger picture now seemed complete; we would be facing it together.

Peru had not only been a demandingly tough physical journey, but a mental and spiritual one as well. Knowing that our future was with each other, we couldn't wait to go and experience it.

Go! Do it:
Take a moment to close your eyes and visualise the time in your life when you were at your most fulfilled.

What is your magical moment? Think about all the factors that contributed to make it special. Breaking through barriers to achieve goals is a liberating experience.

Metaphorically, what is the mountain you want to climb? What is your Everest?

What are the first steps towards conquering it?

Chapter Seven

Fires and Festivities

Jim

Bon air

'Most men pursue pleasure with such breathless haste that they Hurry past it.'
Kierkgaard

It was a bad idea of my fiancée to buy the chocolate-coated coffee beans in the departure lounge as a Peruvian keepsake. The idea of souvenirs for friends and family was a good one. Allowing me to sample them wasn't. By the time we boarded the plane my palms were sweating. The caffeine hit me squarely between the eyes and I felt like flapping my arms and flying to the Bahamas myself.

"Will you try and get some sleep at least?" muttered Emma, tapping a hand adorned with her new engagement ring, on my leg. "Please get some rest, you're becoming unbearable."

"I'm restless" I replied. I tried to expend some of this surplus energy and took to reading about our destination, part of the Lesser Antilles, in the in-flight magazine, *Bonaire*.

As the flight map flashed to show that we were over Venezuela, I asked "Couldn't we afford the better Antilles, and are we flying into a hurricane waiting to happen?"

"Hurricane season finished last month, Katrina has long gone - and you've replaced it. Keep still will you, I need to rest."

Rest wasn't an option after popping those coffee beans. The best I could do to still my chattering mind was to scribble down notes of how I felt after our trip to Peru. It had been everything I'd hoped for. I had:

1) Completed Macchu Picchu.
2) Survived an 11-hour horse trek, and was still walking.
3) Avoided major food poisoning.
4) Found my soul mate with whom I intended to spend the rest of my life.

It had been an amazing experience and, in all honesty, was perhaps less about achievement and more about the reality of a third-world nation, of the simplicity of northern Peru compared with the tourist driven southern area. When I went out, I thought I was a fit Western bloke but found that in comparison to the tour guides, my physical accomplishment amounted to very little.

GO! Think:
How often do you compare yourself to others and how does this make you feel?

Emma

'Challenges make you discover things about yourself that you never Really knew. They're what make the instrument stretch – what makes you go Beyond the norm.'
 Cicely Tyson

After the gruelling expeditions in Peru, the peace and tranquillity of Bonaire was just what we needed. We arrived in the early hours of the morning and as our apartment was on the beach we headed for the sea before even thinking about sleep. The moon was not quite full, but still large enough to spread its iridescent glow over the very still ocean.

Jim

By day, the sea was a rich turquoise, looking as if it had been painted for a travel agent's advert, but it was the clearness of the water that was so startling. Every boat moored in the shallow waters created a shadow that danced on the seabed in the swell.

We strolled hand in hand along the coastline of this fantasy island, enjoying the sea air, blue skies, colourful coral and parrot fish, which were literally an arm's length away. There were two sets of locals; the home grown, island variety and the imported, retired Dutch. One group had been brought up to serve and the latter had worked hard to be waited on. Both, just as we did, had access to the same sun, sand and sea that boasted the best snorkelling and diving in the Caribbean. For the time being, the island felt like our own as we blended into the moment and enjoyed the 'right here, right now.'

GO! Read
The Power of Now, Eckhart Tolle.

Emma

It was one thing snorkelling in water in the daylight where you could see what was around you, but quite another in the dark. After an initial introduction to the shallow black waters of the harbour with the aid of a strong flashlight, we felt brave enough to venture further out of our depth towards the pier.

This was something that was outside my comfort zone; gone was the crystal turquoise sea and in its place was inky black expanse. What was under there? Especially at night. What creatures came out of their lairs to prey on unsuspecting tourists? I soon forgot my fears as I became enthralled at what appeared to be the secret life of the sea; shrimp with pink glowing eyes as our torches sought out their hiding places, octopus and lobster keeping a watchful eye on the moving lights and moray eels entwined around the rocks baring their teeth. The luminous phosphorescence of the algae in the deep waters all around us was a surprising, but fitting, finale to our evening soirée; every movement of hand or foot caused the water to glow around us.

It was an enlightening brief adventure that highlighted how different a place can be when the sun sinks below the horizon. It was a complete hidden world that we do not think about because we have never seen or experienced it. How many other aspects of life could this be applied to? How often do we look beyond the 'norm' of everyday life to see its other side? In Dubai, people seemed too wrapped up in their own existences, to stop to think about the labourers who were helping to physically build the dream. The conditions of the facilities in which they live are often very poor, the food seemed barely edible and they are away from their families for up to three years at a time, yet how many of us stop to consider this when reading about the dream that is being built?

GO! Think:
What would make you step out of your comfort zone?

Jim

As Emma and I meditatively toasted ourselves on the powdery shore among the leather-skinned locals, Em became increasingly inquisitive about Thailand.

"What's the plan?" she enquired as she smothered my freckly shoulders with factor 30.

"OK. Two words: colonic irrigation."

"What?" there was a momentary pause in the cream application.

"That's the script. Seriously. At the health spa we'll be fasting for over a week and getting well and truly flushed out. We end up all fresh-faced to be married on the beach." Well, she *did* ask.

Emma

Colonic irrigation ... aaagh! For one blissful moment, I thought he was joking, but it soon became apparent that he was serious. My romantic thoughts of being pampered for a week in a Thai spa vanished and was replaced by images of long hose pipes and pots of Vaseline. How could he even think of being in Thailand and not taste all that wonderful food?

After letting the thoughts settle for a few minutes I surprised myself by liking the idea. It would be a clean fresh beginning to our marriage, that's for sure. I would be creating a clear space to start married life - literally.

"Hmmm, very symbolic I guess. At least I'll have no worries about fitting into my dress."

GO! Think:
What is important for you about clearing your space both emotionally and physically?

Casi NO!

'Man is a gaming animal. He must always be trying to get the better in Something or other.'
Charles Lamb

After our previous visits to casinos in South Africa and France we were in profit. Bonaire, for all its tranquillity and calm, housed one laidback casino. No dress code, no passport, no blood test was required to gamble here. The place was full of red faces poking out of Hawaiian shirts, deck shoes with no socks, Rolex watches, cigars and strong aftershave.

Within an hour, I'd doubled my money and was determined to treble it.

"What's the point, Babe, we've beaten the system so let's leave it at that, shall we?" suggested Emma as we watched the roulette ball land on my Chester house number, 13, for the second time, bringing me 36 more two dollar royal blue chips.

I'd continued, transfixed on the green baize cloth for a further two hours with Emma patiently waiting, wafting away cigar smoke from her tired eyes.

"Can we per-lease GO! Now?" she tutted.

"Good call," I said as I signalled to the croupier that I'd be cashing in my win.

"It's the right call, Jim you've done well. Enough now." Replied my fiancée cum therapist.

As we cashed up we declined the offer of free booze in a bid to get us to stay longer. Then a punter, the source of the cigar smoke, stacked five hundred dollars' worth of chips on black as the croupier called 'no more bets'. I noticed how big gamblers like that were totally expressionless, regardless of whether they were winning or not. The two dollar highs and lows were enough for me. Provided the punters were watching the wheel spin, turning over their Black Jack hand or fiddling with their chips it was their spare time, their release and their choice The ball plopped on red and the punter squashed his cigar out in the ashtray and promptly left the building.

We treated ourselves to a cab ride back and I vowed that it was my last pop at roulette and was stopping while I was on the up. The next day our one hundred dollars windfall was invested on a day aboard *Woodwind*, a well-equipped catamaran with all the fish, sun and turquoise sea we could handle and a bottle of chilled Chardonnay. Our laid back hosts, complete with their 5 and 8 year old kids, had sailed all over the world and home schooled their children as they sailed.

My third glass made me miraculously remember that we only live once and a return visit to the casino to play with our winnings was a good idea. The previous night's luck was not with me. I miserably frittered away our last dollars.

I could have done without our 30-minute walk of shame back to our hotel but that was the price of gambling away the taxi fare. I now appreciated what Mr five hundred dollars had felt like the night before. Our last morning on the beach was spent snorkelling away my regret between watching parrot fish and collecting smooth shards of blue and green glass that, according to Emma would 'look great in a bowl'. The tranquil shores of Bonaire helped soften my remorse as we relieved the beach of some of the surplus glass before clinking off to England for Christmas.

Emma
Christmas lights and London madness

'We don't live in a world of reality, we live in a world of perceptions.'
Gerald J Simmons

Leaving our island paradise, I did not have the usual feeling of regret, but rather a growing excitement at what was in store when we arrived back in the UK. I had spent the last nine years celebrating Christmas in the Middle East, where 25th December consists of a BBQ around at a friend's villa as the rest of Dubai carries on regardless. I was looking forward to soaking up the atmosphere in the London frenzy, followed by the relaxed pace of life in a sleepy Devon village, in front of a roaring log fire.

Peru was over and so was the Bahamas. We were heading back to normality, whatever and wherever that was. The experiences and memories of the past two months would stay with me forever, shaping my thoughts, rationale and beliefs in the future. I felt that I wanted to make a mountain of changes 'tomorrow' but this wouldn't be realistic and anyway, what would the changes be? It was all very well looking at the simple life of a rural Peruvian family, but that was their life and how they lived it. Among other things Peru *had* made me look at the meaning of contentment and how you can find it in your life whatever you are doing.

GO! Think:
Picture a time in your life when you were fully content. Who are you in this moment?

GO! Read
Oh, The Places You'll Go, Dr Seuss

Jim

Capital idea

'Heap on more wood! The wind is chill; but let it whistle as it will.

   We'll keep our Christmas merry still'
   Sir Walter Scott

Braving London's congestion charge, we drove across the icy cold capital through Piccadilly Circus, over to my brother's, Richard, in the East End. That evening, we commandeered the roaring fireplace at his local pub. With a cask ale in hand, Christmas music blaring out and office parties in full swing we were warming up nicely for Christmas.

"So, congratulations on the engagement. How were the travels then, Emma?" he asked.

"Where do we start?" The last thing I wanted to do was to bore the lad.

We were wary of coming back as intrepid, but boring, explorers. We'd done so much, we both struggled to know where to begin. Besides, we knew from experience that those who have not shared your experience are rarely as interested in it as you are.

Emma

'How many things I can do without.'
   Socrates

I felt like a child again being taken to London and treated to a tour of all the famous sights. We revisited Big Ben, Westminster, Buckingham Palace, Hyde Park, and then travelled through Kensington to Harrods. We finished up in Oxford Street and Regent Street catching a glimpse of the famous Christmas lights before heading off to the East End.

Having grown up in Devon I had always looked on London as somewhere out of my reach. It was where most of the news happened, where all the famous people lived and where the glossy magazines were created. In my imagination, London occupied a country in its own right and was totally inaccessible and separate from the rest of the UK. And here I was, travelling through the heart of it at Christmas time. After all we had been through in the last few months, it seemed a little unreal, but then, what was reality anyway? Peru with its isolated mountain regions, or London in the build-up to Christmas? The only way I could make any sense of it was to think of reality as being wherever I was now.

GO! Think:
What is your reality?

Assailed by the lights, the neon, the bustle and the energy of the city it was easy to forget the hardships we had recently witnessed. I was frustrated that the feelings of these experiences were ebbing away as London barged its way into my thinking and staged a coup on my consciousness. All the same, having been deprived of a UK Christmas for the previous nine years, I felt that London was just adding fuel to the fire of my excitement. So, over the next five days, in the run up to Christmas, I resolved to absorb every piece of atmosphere possible.

The shopping crowd on Oxford Street was a writhing sea of people, wrapped up against the cold. I was freezing cold but loved it. There were enough lights and glitter to decorate the

Fires and Festivities

whole of Lapland. As wonderful as it was, I couldn't help thinking whether the kids in Peru would even have a Christmas stocking let alone be putting anything into it. It was all quite overwhelming.

Even the coffee had cinnamon added, and had been repackaged and sold as a special Christmas blend. Being in the UK during the run up to Christmas, which by all accounts now started at the end of September, I could understand why some people had become so disillusioned with the whole thing. Still, for someone who had not had anything to do with it until 24 hours previously, as I had, I was in heaven. But it was fast turning into a battle of my conscience: the simplicity of Peru versus the commercialism of Christmas here in the UK.

And so it continued until we found ourselves outside Hamleys. We were sucked into the vortex of people snaking their way around the one-way system that had been imposed to deal with the vast numbers. Before we were able to peel off from the conveyor belt and take a breath, we found ourselves on the first floor. I couldn't believe it; Jim's face had lit up like a Christmas tree or, more correctly, like a little boy in a toy-shop.

Jim

I was completely caught up in a world of my own in that toy shop. Not knowing which way to turn I left myself be swept along with the crowds. I was parted from Emma and ended up in the games section where time stood still. I indulged, pressed, blew bubbles and tested everything on offer. There was nothing for it but to buy some entertainment for Christmas. It looked like most of the fathers were enjoying the experience more than their kids whom they had used as an excuse for visiting the place.

Emma

Putting any female's shopping skills in the shade, Jim had spotted, chosen and paid for two large items before I had time to notice that he had even disappeared.

"Where did you go?" I asked, relieved that I had managed to find him after a ten minute absence. Then I noticed the bulging bags.

"Just a little something to keep us entertained over Christmas. After all, we have to have some games to play," he replied, too sheepishly for my liking. And what had prompted this sudden love of shopping? I peeked into the red and gold carrier bag and found a poker set and a roulette wheel, complete with table overlay and gaming chips.

The commercialism of Christmas was screaming from every shop we visited, turning the business of giving into bottom line profit. I felt that the spirit of giving had been truly forgotten.

It was time to retreat to our country farmhouse in South Devon.

GO! Think:
If you could give a gift to humanity, what would it be?

Jim

Christmas Farmhouse

'The perfect Christmas tree? All Christmas trees are perfect!'
    Charles N Barnard

We negotiated the narrow driveway of our hired farmhouse laden with warm clothes for five nights, a couple of cases of wine to be mulled and a cardboard box full of ancient Christmas decorations. Nestled in the rolling hills and dense woodland was the sleepy hideout we'd dreamt of. Two old barns had been joined together and converted into a modern dwelling, complete with slate roof, skylights, heated stone floors, open fireplaces and a modern kitchen.

"It's just perfect," announced Em as she wound reels of fairy lights around the banister.

"Magic, but I don't think we'll be needing that box of decorations, Love," I said as I poked my head round the back of the fireplace.

"This is just the start. We've so much more. Wait till I've finished and decorated a real Christmas tree."

"What do you think that eight-foot thing is in the corner. A hologram?" I said, pointing in disbelief to an artificial decorated tree.

"But it's not real. It's got to *smell* like Christmas."

"What's the point? Buy some pine-scented air freshener instead."

"Good point. We'll need some for the loos. Nine people sharing two bathrooms mean we'll need it."

"And, it's a waste for just a week," I added opening a box of firelighters and a couple of nets full of kindling that were slumped at the side of the fireplace.

"Come on now, Mr. Christmas Spirit."

GO! Read
Christmas Carol by Charles Dickens

Having knotted newspaper and built a wigwam of kindling I needed something more substantial for the fire. I went out gathering bundles of firewood before dusk fell and left Em with the decorations. Scrambling down the leafy lanes, strewn with holly bushes, oak trees and kissing gates I was enjoying things that Dubai lacked: nature, cold air and wildlife. Within an hour our chimney had smoke pouring out of it and as I was about to uncork our first bottle of red wine, I went to hunt for glasses.

"Not yet, Matey," Em snatched the bottle out of my hand and set it on the counter top.

"What? It *is* Christmas. Where is your Christmas spirit?" I shrieked.

"No way. It's time for a real Christmas tree. Come on, let's go before it gets too dark.'

I surrendered the bottle opener too and went to look for my coat. Local gypsies in this part of the world were reputed to offer the best stock of Christmas trees so we headed off towards Dartmoor.

The oversized tree that we ended up with almost required its own trailer. At least seven feet high in its stockinged feet, it filled the back of our little hatchback so there was no room for the extra logs I had hoped to be able to pick up at the same time.

Emma

'Supply always comes on the heels of demand'
　　Robert Collier

The farmhouse was the perfect Christmas house. Nestled in the dip of a valley at the end of a private road it promised peace and quiet, amazing views of the valleys and the promise of country walks through the woods on the edge of the property. Mum, Ken and Aunt Sally, my Godmother arrived in two cars.

"Cooey!" I heard coming from the back seat under what seemed to be a box of cooking utensils.

"You'll have to help me out or I will be here for the whole of Christmas. Your mother insisted on bringing the kitchen with her," chuckled Aunt Sally emerging like a butterfly from her cocoon of pots and pans.

"What a view," came Aunt Sally's seal of approval. "We'll be needing to walk off all your mother's wonderful cooking with what she has planned."

And with that we settled in front of the fire enjoying each other's company and our new surroundings.

Later that evening, Andrew and Ruth stormed down the lane

towards us in their Land Rover. It was packed to the gunwales with cool boxes, chocolates, bottles, cake tins and several suitcases.

Andrew has inherited Mum's love of cooking, so my offer to unload the car had the ulterior motive of investigating what goodies and gastronomic surprises he had in store. I wasn't disappointed: chocolate-covered Florentines, game terrine, cheese straws and jars of ripe tomato chutney. As much as my mouth was watering at the thought of the taste experience that was awaiting us over the next few days, I was feeling uneasy after experiencing such simplicity in Peru. Was this excess really needed in order to celebrate ?

"What on earth?" I gasped as Andrew staggered by with a portable TV and video.

"Don't ask. This is just in case we miss something of national importance and can video it!" he replied nodding his head over in Ruth's direction.

"I like to have my home comforts, especially over Christmas," grinned Ruth as she walked by with a handful of hangers of coats and skirts that would have filled my wardrobe for a month.

The Peruvians would have been speechless. What seems important to them, would seem trivial to us in our privileged lives. Yet what seems important to us, would seem like frivolity, sheer extravagance or pure greed to them. I realised I was heading for an interesting week of learning to live together and accept everyone for who they are.

Jim's parents arrived on Christmas Eve and were a little perplexed when a crowd of us ran out to help unload.

"Er, no need," said Gus. "You're alright." He reached into the back seat and emerged with one large sports bag.

"Well, I suppose you could take this for me," said Marge, stepping lightly from the passenger seat and putting a cardboard box of homemade goodies into my arms. This was the sum total of their luggage.

GO! Think:
What baggage are you carrying around?

My fears were groundless. It turned out to be a wonderful, idyllic Christmas, combining the excitement of childhood with the enjoyment of being an adult. Peru had enabled me to see Christmas through childlike eyes again; the tin of chocolates on the coffee table now seemed decadent. We were cocooned in our own little valley with close family, great food, perfect winter weather and a roaring log fire. Woodland or coastal walks went some way to counteracting the effects of the Christmas fare, giving us all a healthy glow. We all took turns to cook, making it feel like Christmas Day every day. Jim, after several smashes and near fatalities in the kitchen, was banished to the lounge to tend to the fire.

Jim

'The family is one of nature's masterpieces'
George Santayana

"Guess I'll have a can of Boddingtons instead then," I hurrumphed. "You'll miss me when I'm gone."

"But the china won't," June called.

"Hey June, I'd prefer it if you postponed abusing me until after I am your son-in-law, if that's OK?" I grinned and returned to my fire.

"Are you glad we got the second tree now, Jim?" Em asked as she re-arranged the presents around the tree.

"These tree lights are flickering, Jim, can you fix them?" asked June as she brought in a tray of tea, homemade shortbread and a tin of *Quality Street*.

"Stand well back folks," joked Dad, "watch Jim with electricity. He'll be across the room in a flash," he laughed topping up his pint glass with real ale.

"Not more abuse," I mumbled, resisting the urge to fiddle with the lights and beginning, instead, a search for a chocolate-covered toffee.

"Budge up, Jim," June moved in to sit beside me. "And you sit down too, Emma." She said, patting the space next to her. "Tell us about your travels. You must have some wonderful stories"

"Well it was an adventure for sure. Where do we start?" I replied.

"Start by pouring Emma and I a lovely drink. Would you, like a glass of wine," she chuckled.

"They used to believe that evergreen trees would ward off evil spirits and ghosts in medieval days, you know?" Aunty Sally informed us as she peered over *The Guardian* with her half-moon glasses.

"Best get another tree planted then son, your mother's still here," chuckled Dad.

Christmas Eve arrived along with midnight mass and carol singing. Another outdoor patrol followed as we ventured out into thick darkness. On our way to church we dived into the local pub where we enjoyed a couple of pints of scrumpy cider in front of the log fire. Our lateness for the service didn't stop the locals acknowledging us as we tiptoed into the last pew in the church, right at the back. A feeling of Christmas contentment and belonging flooded me.

GO! Think:

How often do you stop to enjoy the feelings of utter contentment and wellbeing in our fast paced world?

How can you know what gives you this feeling if you don't stop to acknowledge it?

Emma

A Cool Yule

'Aren't we forgetting the true meaning of Christmas? You know, the birth of Santa?'
Bart Simpson

Having the family gathered around the meal table for a whole week was wonderful; no one had to rush out to go to work or do anything. Conversation flowed as freely as the wine, with plenty of laughter and celebrations. The Christmas dinner itself, cooked by Mum, with Andrew as sous chef, was the best I have ever tasted and far out-stripped any memories of childhood Christmases. But maybe it is always like that.

GO! Read
The Night Before Christmas, Clement Clarke Moore

Jim

"So what about the wedding day then?" asked June. "Get some more gravy Jim and help yourself to another Yorkshire pudding."

Emma squeezed my hand. My cue to talk. "Well … it'll just be a very simple ceremony on the beach in Thailand."

"What about family coming?" she asked.

"Well, you know what it's like, you invite one and you've got to cater for them all." Forgetting I was speaking to my future mother-in-law, she rightly continued, open mouthed with "What, no family?"

Emma jumped in with "The wedding ceremony is more of a seal of our travels, Mum but more importantly we see this Christmas as the main celebration."

"Really?" Asked her mum, reaching for a tissue.

"It is the only time that both families will be together," added Emma.

As June looked at me for reassurance, I added, "So basically, it is just Em and me, that's it." I felt compelled to tell it as it was but on reflection I could have been a little more sensitive.

The sound of June's knife and fork dropping on to her plate made us both look up mid-mouthful. Taking care to fold her napkin and replace it on the table, June then headed for the kitchen without meeting our eyes. That was Em's cue to follow her out, taking a box of tissues with her. I guess some spin could have softened the blow but this was the wedding we wanted.

"It's a double celebration this Christmas, Mum, and we wouldn't want it any other way," reassured Em again as she offered June another tissue, her re-heated dinner pinged in the microwave. She dealt with the situation wonderfully and I was eventually back in favour, helping load up the car for our early morning recce down to South Hams.

Emma

I had started planning for Christmas months in advance but was not sure whether the reality would live up to the dream. But it had surpassed it, especially with the celebrations of our engagement to add to the festivities.

We had planned a big family Christmas but gained so much more than just the celebration. The time we had together created wonderful memories that we would treasure, not knowing when we would get the chance to repeat the experience. Secretly, I was already planning a repeat performance in a few years' time in our own property that we had yet to find, with the two dogs that we had yet to rescue.

Jim

"Merry Christmas everyone and congratulations to Emma and Jim," announced June raising the glass of Monbazillac that accompanied the flaming pudding. Our engagement was toasted and our Peruvian weight loss began to feel like a distant memory.

"So what's next for you two then?" asked Aunty Sally, "when you're married?"

"Well ...." I looked at Em, adjusting my brand new chocolate brown socks.

"We'll see how we feel. Maybe UK, maybe south of France, maybe Dubai?"

"Maybe even Thailand."

Sally had a point. What was next for us? A wave of panic shuddered through me as the realisation of no job, no place to live and no routine dawned on me. Surely that was the whole point of travelling? Was it the exploration, the uncertainty and the blessing of sharing it with someone I wanted to grow old with? Whatever the next step was I'd be sharing it with Emma.

GO! Think:

What is next for you?

*Bye-**Bye** 05*

'Cheers to a new year and another chance for us to get it right.'
   Oprah Winfrey

Back up in Chester, Dad said that there would be the usual New Year celebrations and that we'd be welcome to join them if we could handle indulging in vol-au-vents, more Christmas cake and mince pies.

"Happy New Year," the four of us toasted as Big Ben chimed midnight on BBC 2. There were no New Year resolutions this year as my last one had been never to make any again. Dad did his usual disappearing act, leaving the house through the back door at one minute to 12 and entering through the front (having rung the bell) just after midnight. A lot had happened that year, I had resigned from work, left Dubai, travelled and got to know Em, finishing up with a proposal. What the next year had in store for us remained to be seen. But whatever it was, I was looking forward to it.

GO! Think:

Imagine it is New Year's Eve and you have to make one resolution to transform your life. What resolution would you make and what impact would it have?

Emma

Back to reality?

'We shall not cease from exploration, and the end of all our exploring Will be to arrive where we started and know the place for the first time.'
T S Eliot

Dubai beckoned en route to Thailand and promised a crazy week of sorting out red tape before we flew on to Thailand. Before leaving Dubai earlier, we had been invited to attend the wedding of Jim's ex managing director, Dick, whose nuptials had been planned, only two days after our return.

We were soon back to the champagne lifestyle city, which was worlds away from Peru, and Devon too. Not even London could compare. Rich in art, culture and heritage, London at least had the advantage of being one of the oldest capitals in the world. Dubai was at the other end of the scale, young in terms of its history with new streets and road systems appearing in our absence. A young city, populated by people from the full range of life; those who can afford to take advantage of the luxury and opulence on offer, and those who lived in the poverty of labour camps and overcrowded accommodation. Still, we had to remember that Dubai was a land of opportunity.

Jim

So, back from whence we came. As our taxi headed down the glass clad Sheik Zayed Road it was as though we picked up exactly where we left off despite this city refusing to stand still. I was amazed at how quickly construction was progressing as we weaved in and out of the temporary access roads that cut in between brand new partially clad buildings directed by sweat-drenched Indian labourers in their faded blue overalls. These guys put their lives on the line waving their little red flags like railway guards with only traffic cones to keep them safe. Safe enough to send money back home to keep families fed and watered.

Tower blocks had grown up and webs of more courageous workers still clung onto the scaffolding. Over a quarter of the world's cranes were now deployed here and as the taxi took us on roads that had been desert just eight months earlier we appreciated the relentless progress that had gone on in our absence.

"Home sweet home, my love," I chuckled as we peered across at the world's tallest tower, Burj Dubai, which had now reached its fortieth floor. 180 floors were planned and it was rumoured to become 800 metres high. Throw into the mix a serious bid for the 2020 Olympics, the largest shopping centre in the world and the opening of an indoor ski dome, it was clear that Dubai was progressing as relentlessly as ever. Whatever would the villagers of Peru make of all this?

GO! Read
Telling tales : An Oral history of Dubai, Julie Wheeler & Paul Thuysbaert

As I opened the door of my old flat that was now 'ours' I was relieved to find that all the furniture was still intact. You can never be sure with tenants. But my pleasure turned to fear when I saw the letter from the management company on the floor. They were threatening to evict us if we didn't update them with postdated cheques for 2006. I had no idea how that had happened. My heart sank. This was important. The last thing we wanted was to return from Thailand with no threshold over which to carry my new wife.

"Best get unpacking and I'll need to sort out what we're wearing for Dick and Chris's wedding," announced Em as she peered into the empty fridge. What was she expecting to find in there?

"How about the white thong, red heels and that blue number?" I replied, hanging up a 2006 Calendar.

"That's you sorted out, now what about me?" joked Em, scouring last year's Yellow Pages for a removal firm. We'd left ourselves a couple of days to merge the contents of Em's flat into mine, or ours, as it now was.

"I'm off to sort out this management letter. Eviction was not on my list of things to do."

"Back to reality, Babe, 'chores R us'."

I darted straight to the management office where they apologised for the confusion and explained it was a matter of course to send such letters to all the tenants.

"We are sorry, Mr Jim, we send everyone those letters. They don't mean anything," said the Filipino behind her sweep of mahogany reception desk.

"So we're OK to stay?" I chuckled with relief.

"Act-oo-ally Sir no problem, as long as we record your intent to stay." I wasn't sure where we'd be settling but for the sake of a roof over our heads, I went along with it and signed.

Emma

Wedding celebrations

'The goal in marriage is not to think alike, but to think together.'

Will Stanton

There were so many things to do on arriving that much to Jim's amusement, I found myself writing a 'to do' list.

With my list of jobs written down, I prioritised the tasks, feeling myself slowly wind up a gear in preparation for the onslaught of the Dubai pace of life. That was until something stopped me in my tracks: the ruler of Dubai had tragically died a few hours before our plane touched down.

Handing in Jim's suit to be pressed for the wedding in a day or two we asked to have an express service.

"Sorry madam that is not possible as we will be closed tomorrow," came the reply. "But you are always open on a Thursday or have I got my days mixed up?" I genuinely doubted myself.

"That's right madam. But we are closed for mourning time. Seven days. Sheikh Maktoum died this morning"

In Dubai, when the ruler, or an important Sheikh dies, the country enters into a period of mourning where everything grinds to a halt. Shops, banks and schools close as well as all government departments. Sheikh Maktoum had been a well-respected and revered ruler whose sudden death from a heart attack at the age of 63 had sent shock waves through this usually vibrant city. He was a gentle man, who had shied away from the spotlight, happy to take a back seat in ruling Dubai alongside his brother Mohammed Hamdan. Sheikh Mohammed had been a figurehead of Dubai and was now assumed to succeed as the new ruler, taking away any fear of unrest among Dubai's local and expat population.

A week of mourning was announced in his honour.

GO! Think:
What do you want to achieve before you die? At your funeral, what will people say about you?

Dick and Chris's wedding thankfully went ahead, despite the

period of mourning that also meant no parties and no live enter-tainment. We were very excited about meeting up with friends that we had not seen for over six months. But getting to the ceremony was a test in itself. I had lost the ability to get ready in a hurry. I thought I had given myself plenty of time, but I ended up being hustled out of the door, hopping as I tried to put my shoes on with jewellery and lipstick still to apply in the car.

"I can't believe you are still not ready, all you had to do was wash your hair," said Jim, incredulous, when he came back from a game of golf to find me still walking around in my dressing gown, not realising it had taken me nearly half an hour to re-acquaint myself with the iron and press his suit myself.

"I know, it's ridiculous, but I had forgotten how long it takes to do hair and make up properly. I am well and truly out of practice," I replied as I struggled to put my earrings in without smudging my nails.

Jim

'All weddings are similar but every marriage is different.'
John Berger

The ceremony ran flawlessly until, during the vows, a mobile phone rang. Heads shook in disgust and a murmur ran through the aisles. I wondered if the vicar would reprimand the guilty party as the ring tone got louder. The phone continued ringing until the vicar reached under his cassock, retrieved his mobile phone and finally switched it off. It was priceless and full credit to the married couple who took it all in their stride as the vicar shrugged with embarrassment.

My ex-colleague, John, who now owned a Thailand hotel, was best man and, remembering his antics in the office, I looked forward to his speech.

Prior to picking up his microphone John took me to one side.

"Everything OK with your wedding plans?" asked John.

"Yep, we're all set."

"Look. I've been thinking, if you fancy a stint running the hotel when you get back, to flex your marketing muscles, then be my guest. You two would be perfect for the place." He flatteringly added that he required a couple he could not only trust but who would also be able to shape the business.

"Not sure where we're going to be in a couple of months, John but we'll certainly give it some thought," I replied, touched by his faith in us. It was another option for us to consider and gave us reason not to drop our anchor too hastily.

"Must dash," John said, stubbing out his cigar and excusing himself. "I'm on."

"Being his best man is like sleeping with the queen ..." he started.

"... it's an honour to be asked but no-one really wants to do it".

Emma

Preparations for new beginnings

'I trust Jim one hundred per cent – except where garlic, coffee or chili are involved'
Emma Wheat

Our final preparation was for the spa. When Jim made the booking back in the internet café in France, he also received some pre-spa instructions. We were encouraged to stick to a diet of fruit and vegetables, cut out the tea and coffee (hence our last sacrificial coffee the night before) and drink a daily glass of a liver flush drink, which would help us maximise the effects of our visit.

GO! Discover Liver flush drink:
1½ tablespoons of olive oil

1 clove of garlic
1 small piece of ginger
1 capsule of cayenne
1 teaspoon fresh lime juice
1½ cups of orange juice

Jim, in his enthusiasm, made the drink for us, but I had forgotten about his love of garlic and spice. I have heard of husbands poisoning their wives after several years of marriage, but never before the marriage even begins. It took a split second for my brain to recognise the sourness of the lime and the pungent taste of garlic before the heat of the cayenne exploded in my mouth. My eyes nearly jumped from their sockets and my tongue tried desperately to escape the usual safety of my mouth. So when my breathing had returned to normal and the shock had worn off I tried to find out what had gone wrong.

"Did the spa send you this recipe or did you make it up?" I spluttered, trying not to dampen his enthusiasm.

"No, I followed the recipe, but doubled the amount, so that we would have enough for tomorrow morning. It's got a bit of a kick hasn't it?" he replied, grinning.

"When you say 'doubled the recipe' what exactly did you do?"

Go! Read
Juicing for Health, Caroline Wheater

Eventually Jim admitted that he had not strictly followed the recipe and his version went something like this:

5 tablespoons of olive oil ('it's good for you, so thought I'd add a bit extra'),

1 piece of garlic (one piece being one *bulb*),

1 large piece of ginger (about four inches long 'ginger's good

for you too'),

1 capsule of cayenne (no capsule and still using the table-spoon, so one tablespoon)

1 teaspoon fresh lime juice ('we didn't have any oranges for the juice so I used all the limes' - about six).

No wonder it literally took my breath away. I was more than happy to stick to the diet of fruit and vegetables during the build-up to the spa, but I decided to wait until I got there before I tried any more miracle drinks that would give me the perfect body. With my mind at rest over the apartment and my body ready for the spa, my soul was looking forward to the tranquillity that lay ahead.

Thailand here we come.

Go! Do it:
Accept people for who they are not what they have or what they do.

1. Write down five people that you can count on in your life. Who would help you in any situation?

2. Some people have lots of money but little time to enjoy it, others have little money but plenty of time to enjoy things. Which one is wealthy?

3. Write two headings on a page:
   Time and Money.
   Write the impact on your life of not having enough of either time or money.
   What is more important to you, time or money?

Chapter Eight

Thai-ing the Knot

Emma

Fantasy Thailand

'Your work is to discover your work and then with all your heart give yourself to it.'
   Buddha

Less than a year ago, Jim and I hadn't admitted to each other, let alone to anyone else, that we were even in a relationship. Back then, I had felt truly independent for the first time since leaving university. I had bought my own flat, was watching my hard-earned salary go into my bank account every month and was able to make my own decisions without having to consult anyone first. I loved every minute of being a free and single woman and would never have imagined that less than a year later, I would be heading off on a plane to get married, quietly on a beach in Thailand. Without any family or friends. What was I doing?

Of course, I knew exactly what I was doing. And I had no second thoughts, despite what I might be trading in. Being with Jim seemed both the most natural and the most exciting thing in the world. The key to our relationship was letting each other be the person with whom we had each fallen in love. We gave each other space to do our own thing as and when we needed to. And that to me, meant I didn't feel I was giving up my independence.

Getting married quietly, and alone, seemed the right thing to do too. Our six months of travel had been about Jim and I doing things very simply. And the wedding was undoubtedly the pinnacle of that. I love my family, but did not want to worry about them having to get to Thailand, or about whether they would enjoy it. Was this selfish? To this day, I don't know. But this was about us two, together, alone and the symbolism of what we were doing.

Jim

'Do not use elevator, while causing fire.'
A sign in an elevator in a Thailand hoteL

Despite our initial scepticism it looked as though Megalopolis Dubai was going to succeed in its ambitious development plans. The Aussie captain of our flight invited us to look down from our Bangkok-bound 747 at the progress of *The World;* the artificial island with most of its 200 sandy islands now visible.

"I remember when all this was just sea," I commented, wondering what the view would be like in five years' time. But what about our world? Where would *we* be, doing what and with whom? For the next few weeks, at least, it was to be centred in Thailand.

GO! Read
The World is Flat, Thomas Friedman.

Emma

The humidity of Bangkok enveloped us the moment we stepped out of the airport. Driving through the congested traffic, I was soon reminded what a city of contrasts this was. Tall, shiny new buildings rose arrogantly from the ground next to old, crumbling, dirty-fronted neighbouring buildings cowering in their shadow. In contrast, Bangkok's mass transport system, Sky Train, which has dominated the landscape since 1999 is a futuristic, electric train that is accurately run to the second by faceless technology. Its ugly, grey, concrete columns blocked the sunlight from the street below that was still choked with hundreds of cars constantly churning out clouds of grey fumes.

Expensive cars jostled with tuk-tuks and people on bikes, trying to make a meagre living peddling all types of food from deep fried bugs to more appetising chicken wrapped in pandan leaf. Buddhist monks in vivid orange robes would occasionally appear in the melée and walk by silently, oblivious. Beggars sat outside shopping centres, ignored by the shoppers with designer shopping bags who simply stepped round them before hailing their tuk-tuk to take them home.

Jim

At our hotel at Soi 33, off Sukhumvit Road, the receptionist greeted us with the customary *Sawaddee Ka* (hello) and *wai* (bow). Emma returned the compliment, bowing slightly with her palms together, explaining to me how, although foreigners are not expected to initiate the wai gesture, it is an insult not to return it.

We ventured out into the busy evening streets that took us by surprise with an explosion of bright lights, party atmosphere and throngs of revellers.

Emma

The city developed a different persona as the sun set. Street hawkers began cooking up exotic foods to feed the office workers who streamed out of the tall, shiny buildings. Girls, wearing a variety of skimpy black evening dresses, gathered outside most of the bars to entice passers-by inside for a beer, promising them a good time. By the time darkness had fallen, the smells of Bangkok had reached their peak encouraged by the heat of the day. The food, the flower stalls and car fumes mixed intermittently with the overpowering stench of drains.

Jim

This was to be our base for the next five days so that we could register our marriage at the British Embassy and deal with the necessary paperwork. Navigating our way around the place became an art, dodging around traders who filled the bustling streets offering snacks of dried cockroaches, maggots and beetles.

We headed for the Khao San Road markets where the backpackers hang out and where the markets display an exciting range of tropical fruits, some used as props in the nearby bars.

Emma

The night market was a shopper's heaven, boasting over 3,700 stalls set out in a labyrinth of Aladdin's caves selling everything from wooden carvings, incense sticks, cushions sparkling with sequins, jewellery and blissfully, handbags and shoes.

Jim

"They really understand the meaning of 'hospitality' here. Do you fancy a massage yet?" I asked, nudging Emma as we walked past one of the go-go bars. "I'll be back in an hour, Love."

"Cheeky. Best we save ourselves until the spa," she replied, stopping to inspect a carpet roll of Thai silk.

"What on earth is the point?" I asked enviously eyeing a carefree expat taking a lug out of his 500ml bottle of ice-cold Chiang beer.

"Well, we're meant to prepare for our fasting with fruit, water and raw vegetables."

"One beer won't hurt."

"It defeats the object. For our bodies to heal, we need to get used to this fasting business. Sharpish."

"It shouldn't make any difference what massages we have and what we eat between now and when we get to the spa – it'll all be coming out at the spa anyway. Surely that makes for better value for money?"

We settled for watching the hordes of people and the activity around a corner bar that was packed with locals tucking into their green and red Thai curries. This was to be our last square meal before we started our flush-out session so we didn't hold back. I polished off a delicious *Tom Yam Kung* soup – a spicy mixture of lemon grass, chilli, lime, mushroom and shrimp, followed with a Thai red curry with sticky rice, washed down with coconut juice straight from the shell. I wondered what the detox would be like, if I'd be OK and if there would be any adverse side effects after my Western diet and one too many pints of lager.

Beyond that, we stuck to fruit juice and vegetables for the rest of the week and explored the city on foot, by tuk-tuk, taxi and Sky Train to avoid the queues when whizzing back and forth to the British Embassy. We agreed that our beach wedding should at least be recognised by our home country and the British Embassy processed a couple of hundred wedding certificates per week, mainly Western men with Thai brides. Registering as Mr and Mrs Wheat involved inevitable red tape, requiring transla-tions and a formal affirmation. But we finally obtained an ornate certificate for our efforts, bearing an impressive stamp.

Emma
Cleansing more than just the soul

'I am not a vegetarian because I love animals; I'm a vegetarian because I hate plants.'
Whitney Brown

The relentless pace of Bangkok was soon replaced by serenity on the island of Samui where we settled into our teak Royal Suite bungalow and marvelled at the lush tropical coconut plantations of Lamai valley on our very own hillside, nestled between palm trees. The lush greenery, colourful flowers and glimpse of the azure sea was all balm to the soul as we were about to give our bodies a holiday. Cocooned in our own little world, it was easy to see how you could forget about the outside world and concentrate on fasting while enjoying the tranquillity of the surroundings. This was going to be a doddle.

Jim

In our bathroom, neatly arranged, were a surfboard cum sink contraption, a red sieve and a couple of buckets with transparent hosepipes and various sized nozzles clipped on the side.

"Shall we go large?" I asked Emma, holding up the plastic pipe that looked like it belonged to part of a homebrew kit. It was only then that we began to realise what we'd let ourselves in for. This was no holiday.

Emma

"Well Em, what do you think? Will this be OK for the next ten days?" asked a beaming Jim as he leant on the balcony surveying the view below.

"It is beautiful, thank you. I have to say the rose petals on the bed are a very special touch," I replied realising what lengths he had gone to so that everything was perfect.

We found the information packs that were in our room, which outlined the routine over the next week. I studied mine carefully, reading it several times until I understood the daily schedule. Jim skipped through it in his normal speed-reading style and promptly spent the rest of the afternoon interrogating me.

"So when does the fasting start, have you found that out yet?" he queried, hoping that we could have one 'last supper' before the fasting began.

"Well, as you can see on the first line of page one, it tells you exactly when to start.

Are you sure you have read the info?"

'Of course, I was just checking you understood it, that's all. When do we start the colema flushes? That's the one bit I am really not looking forward too, I have to admit.'

'The time and place for our induction video is on page two, half way down, in a separate box, but you would have seen that already, wouldn't you?'

'Induction? What induction? Can't they just leave us to get on with it in the privacy of our bathroom?' he replied, with his eyes nearly popping out on stalks.

"I'm sure they will do once we know what we're doing."

"But I ..." he started

"If you read the information, all your questions will be answered. It is all there," I interrupted as it was now obvious that he had clearly not taken on board any of the information. And from there, to my surprise, he did. For the next week, he did not have his nose out of the book, reading, digesting and regurgitating mountains of nutritional facts that he had never heard before, including some that I wish had lain undiscovered.

"Hey Em, did you know that the average man carries up to five kilos of undigested waste in his body that can stay there for years?"

"No I can honestly say that fact is not in my repertoire of knowledge," I replied.

"And did you know that there are over a 100 different types of parasites that can live inside the human body that lay up to 200,000 eggs a day?" he continued.

"That's not in my knowledge bank either."

Jim

The literature warned that we were embarking on an emotional roller coaster as the body rids itself of negative energy and thoughts, as well as the undigested food. The detox system uses a special warm solution to remove embedded waste and toxins from your large intestine. Undigested matter left in the colon can become toxic over time, you see. Prior to this, mention of things such as my liver, colon and intestines hadn't meant a great deal to me. All of a sudden, I was terrified. What on earth would come out of me after all these years? The curry? The wolfed-down pizzas? Untold chocolate bars, parasites, worms or a golf tee?

GO! Think:
If you could go on an emotional detox, what would you want to get rid of?

Emma

That evening before our induction video, we wandered down to have our last meal at the spa's restaurant before the fast began. And this is where the cruel twist of fate really came into play. The restaurant in this spa had been voted one of the world's top fifty restaurants, according to the *Sunday Times*. What a cruel joke in a place where 50 per cent of the guests are fasting and can only sit and watch others enjoy the delectable cuisine. Fresh market vegetables, cooked in a variety of Thai styles alongside freshly caught seafood; prawns sautéed with lemongrass, garlic and fresh ginger; calamari cooked with tomato and onion or mussels with butter and sweet basil cooked in a steaming pot. How would we last the week?

Jim

Despite me preparing to flush I could have tucked into a hot and spicy pizza there and then. Even though this was my idea in the first place I wondered how we'd get value for money in this resort. Normally I was used to an 'eat all you can' and here we were about to embark on a flush all you can, with the hosepipe included.

Emma

However long we took over our meal, there was no avoiding the dreaded video that awaited us. Jim was like an excited puppy at the thought of all his past misdemeanours with alcohol and other suspect substances being flushed out of his body. I was looking forward to it more out of curiosity and the fact that it promised a substantial weight loss. But we were both horrified to find that the video was shown in the reception area, in full view of everyone. To make matters worse, we were in a small group, with two girls joining us for the induction. Well, I'm British and *we* don't discuss things like this in public. I am not a prude when it comes to most things, but I cannot remember feeling more embarrassed than sitting in the company of two strangers, hearing how I was going to be putting a lubricated tube up my rear end twice a day for the next week. I was just thankful that I would get to do it in the privacy of our bathroom, with no one else around.

Jim

Emma was well aware of the demonstration video running through the basics but I failed to mention the compulsory 'hands on' session with these total strangers. I denied all knowledge.

Emma

And just as I thought it couldn't get any worse, it did. Not satisfied with the video demonstration, we were then given a personal demonstration. But not just with Jim and myself as pupils, the two, large, slightly nervous girls were invited along too. They looked even more mortified than we did. They did not know each other and, just like Jim and I, had hoped for anonymity.

"Right, shall we get started?" asked Denise, who was the member of staff assigned to show us how things worked. "There really is nothing to worry about. Just remember to use plenty of KY jelly and keep the air out of the tube," she continued as though we were conducting a perfectly normal conversation.

Jim

The two girls looked horrified at the mention of KY and I started to smile. Emma glared at me as she realised I was about to launch into my repertoire of slippery jokes.

Emma

Denise assembled the equipment followed by a fully clothed demonstration. I was sure you would need at least two pairs of hands to guide the tube, control the water flow and balance yourself on a board that hovered over the toilet.

"By this time tomorrow, I am sure we will all be happily sharing our experiences," added Jim now keen to get on with it.

With the end of the demonstration and the hasty exit of our two new 'friends,' came the reality of putting all our new-found knowledge into practice. Tomorrow morning, I would be flushing sixteen litres of coffee solution through my body, when I would rather drink it as part of that nice new Starbucks' cinnamon latte concoction.

GO! Think:
What embarrasses you? What is behind the embarrassment?

Jim

The seven-day challenge that lay ahead was listed on a board behind the bar with the names of the clients and what day of the fast they were on. The deal was that we were to check in twice each day, at 7am and 7pm, when we had to jump on the scales, collect our detox supplements and then get through the routine as prescribed with absolutely no cheating. Mai, our Thai server, ticked off our names and served us our first spa cocktail, a heavy tonic of bentonite clay with psyllium husk.

"You must drink quickly sir," Mai instructed as she handed the glass of green mush over to me. "It expands very quickly and then you cannot drink it." Another fellow was having to spoon his feed straight down his throat, as it now resembled porridge. After having forced half of it down he proceeded to throw the rest back up. It was like being back at Nottingham University in the hall bar, but couldn't have been further from those days of debauchery.

"Down the hatch then, love, and happy holidays!" I said, raising my glass to Emma. But I soon realised, that this bright idea of mine was not going to be as simple to carry out as I'd first thought. "Coffee, garlic or bentonite, Sir?" Mai asked taking the sludge-laden cup away from me.

"More drink?" I replied.

"No sir."

"You mean that I'm to have a coffee enema?"

She nodded.

A waste of good coffee, I thought.

"It's the enema solution, it passes through you," giggled Mai.

"No, not coffee. Don't you have decaf? It's better for him," asked a perturbed Emma.

"No ma'am. Organic coffee only. It passes through the easiest," she replied.

"Oh dear," groaned Emma.

"Look, keep your friends close and your enemas ever closer," I laughed. But this was no time for humour.

I did finally opt for coffee, seeing that this was to be my only vice for the next week, though not normally taken this way! Having weighed in we wandered back up to our mountainside retreat amongst the scented purple orchids and tropical fruit trees with our buckets and supplements in hand. Suddenly the path was blocked by a giant of a man, the 350-pound spa veteran, Gus. With his smiling eyes, and ship-wrecked look he stopped for breath, swept his hair back and stretching in his XXL Disneyland tee-Shirt asked:

"You guys here for the first time?"

"What's it like?" asked Emma, bravely.

"Honestly? Well you'll feel fine for a couple of days, then weak and miserable but way better after day six. Just stick with it. Oh, and you never know what you're going to find in that red sieve. Well, my friends, you're encouraged to inspect whatever comes out," he grinned.

"*What?*" asked Emma, choking on her coconut juice.

Emma

I was just about coming to terms with the whole process, until I spoke to Gus. Big mistake. Going through the colonic irrigation was one thing, but I was NOT about to go through the results of it. I was beginning to belong to the school of thought that ignorance was bliss.

Jim

"Well we're all here for the same thing, to get healthy. When I first looked I found something moving in my sieve and I nearly ruptured myself falling off that surfboard contraption. Damned thing ain't designed to take my weight." he laughed, patting his stomach proudly. By this stage Emma had her hand over her mouth and I was wondering if I'd done the right thing bringing my fiancée to this colonic concentration camp.

"Look, it's only parasites and they're not that uncommon. We have all sorts of things going on in our stomach and you're here giving yours a service. I'll let you folks get a good night's rest."

"Ok, thanks for all your advice." I replied sheepishly.

"Hey and don't be shy with the KY." He laughed as we headed back to our suite.

Emma

With equipment at the ready, candles and incense lit (well, you may as well make the most of lying down for half an hour) all I had to do was lie back, relax and enjoy, which strangely, I did. This was the one physical part of the fast that showed instant results.

All I am prepared to share, however is that I came out smiling.

Aside from that, what happened in the bathroom stays in the bathroom. It was now Jim's turn, but seeing that I had survived the experience, he was reassured that it couldn't be too bad. I was just worried about the effect the coffee would have on him. It was bad enough when he drank a cup, let alone flushed sixteen litres of the stuff through himself twice a day. Only time would tell. I would just have to sit back and watch.

Jim

Feeling flush

'The greatest wealth is health.'
  Virgil

I filled up my bucket of coffee and prepared for my first colema just as the sun rose. Ironic really, seeing as I was about to pipe something where the sun didn't shine.

"I hope I can do this bloody flush out, best you keep your distance eh?" I suggested to Emma as I carried a full bucket over to the window ledge next to the toilet and surfboard.

"You'll be fine. Look, I'll leave you in peace, my love and go and check out the spa library. Good luck," she reassured me as she headed back down the path.

My first attempt to flush out was a clumsy one with coffee solution spraying around our bathroom.

Once the nozzle was where it was meant to be, I lay back like a racing driver in the cockpit, taking my weight on my forearms and trying my utmost to relax. A couple of deep breaths later the warm liquid flushed into me as the level of the bucket slowly dropped. Taking in as much solution as possible I rapidly felt I had stomach cramps and had to release. It was like the feeling you get after eating too much, but with a cold sweat thrown in and some vigorous shaking.

Feelings of relief, regret, humiliation and dread came and

went as I focussed on the calming wisps of incense smoke while trying to hold in as much solution for as long as possible. My colonic deposits - years' worth of rotting food lining the walls of my intestine - were caught by the little red sieve for inspection. Thankfully, they didn't appear to be moving and were flushed away just as I was violently sick.

Time stood painfully still during the first three days at the spa as my condition went from lively to downright miserable. First of all I had a nasty dull headache and bloodshot eyes. Then my tongue turned from red to yellow to green and finally to grey. My breath could have stripped paint off the side of a ship. My toxins were coming out – fast - and the spa doctor assured me that this was normal and were just the results of modern-day living. While undergoing the detox, we met people from all sorts of backgrounds. These ranged from drug rehabs to binge eaters, workaholics to health freaks. But who they were didn't matter. We were all on the spa journey together and the labels that society branded us with melted away as quickly as the weight.

GO! Think:
What labels does society put on you?

Emma

Food for thought

'The one way to get thin is to re-establish a purpose in life.'
Cyril Connolly

The first few days were spent doing very little as we barely had enough energy for anything, except enjoying the tranquillity of our surroundings. Each morning we would wake up and watch the sun rise over the coconut groves that led down to the sparkling sea. With the sun came the cockerel chorus from around the valley. As one crowed, another would answer until this was taken over by other sounds: bird song, crickets chirruping and a cacophony of insect noises.

So much for thinking this was going to be easy. The first few days of the fast were the hardest. By the second day, I lay in bed shivering with a toxin-induced fever. My head was pounding and I felt like a recovering alcoholic. I realised what toxins my body must have been trying to expel to make me feel this bad. But once I had broken through this second day, although still very tired, I had what I can only describe as the feeling of being completely renewed.

We soon became masters at our routine of cleansing drinks, herbal supplements and 'colemas' (the name they used for the colonic irrigation routine), which we were now successfully administering twice a day. The tight schedule meant that the time passed quickly and together with a few massages and our morning meditation exercises we soon felt our bodies changing for the better. My skin started to glow and my hair shone. After the days of withdrawal symptoms, headaches and lethargy, I was filled with a new energy, which I wanted to keep after leaving the spa – I just had to find out how.

Jim

By the end of day seven I'd lost more than six kilos of surplus weight and possessed skin that shone, strong nails and pure whites in my eyes. I could even see my cheekbones when I looked in the mirror. I felt like I was 18 years old again. Clarity of thought, a sense of adventure and feeling ready to face whatever lay ahead came to me at once.

We were advised to give our bodies a chance and break our fast with raw foods only for the first two or three days to avoid any adverse reaction. We opted for papaya, bee pollen and goat's milk. Food had never tasted so good and it was taking us 15 minutes to finish our breakfast when only weeks before I would have gobbled it down in no time.

As we were becoming increasingly clear-headed we hired a moped to race around the island to the district office and register our Thai documents in order to become Mr and Mrs Wheat. We left the office with everything signed, sealed and approved but decided to leave the exchanging of rings until our beachside Buddhist blessing a couple of days later.

GO! Read
A Prescription for Nutritional Healing, Phyllis Balch.

Barefoot in Bophut

Emma
'What's a wedding? Webster's dictionary describes it as the act of removing Weeds from one's garden.'
  Homer Simpson

We left the spa with renewed energy and a radiant glow. We had survived the seven day fast feeling refreshed and buzzing with energy, ready to have our marriage blessed by the monks.

  Bophut was a small fishing village on Koh Samui, and was just starting to wake up to the effects of tourism, but had not yet been spoiled like some of the other towns on the island. The beach stretched for about two miles, the entire length of the village with most restaurants placed on the shoreline. Our hotel overlooked part of this beautiful stretch of beach where we were going to be blessed in the shade of a palm tree, with the crystal sea lapping gently at the shore a few feet away. With no menu to finalise or family to organise, it was a very relaxed few days leading up to the event itself.

Jim
We were free to roam wherever we chose, no pills to take, tubes to insert or sieves to inspect. We decided that an organic café was

the place for us to eat and we munched slowly on a pumpkin and baby spinach salad.

"Only a few more days and we'll be able to eat what we like," said Em who smiled as she pointed to the burger and organic fries on a more attractive section of the menu.

"Why can't we just get stuck into a burger now, or at least share one? I could murder one." The thought really did appeal, despite my recent flush and increased knowledge.

"Don't worry there'll be time for a burger or three. All in good time."

Several days of even more rest, relaxation, massages and swimming left us practically glowing for our wedding day. We slowly built back to more substantial foods, sharing a vegetable *pad thai* and coconut juice. I realised that in 48 hours I'd be a married and Buddhist blessed man. Lucy, the bubbly British daughter of John, who was coincidentally also at the spa though based in Dubai, confirmed that they had managed to "hire" three Buddhist monks from the local monastery to preside over things. The only condition was that we made a donation to their cause and provided them with a meal, which would be their only meal of the day.

'You can get everything in life you want if you will just help enough other People get what they want.'
Zig Ziglar

Emma

I would like to say that the morning of the wedding dawned with the sun streaming through the window, but I can't. As Jim leapt out of bed to take a look out, I noticed something different about the light in the room.

"How's it looking out there this morning?" I asked as he peered through a small gap in the curtains, refusing to draw them.

Jim

I was a lucky man. Here was the girl who stood by me and resigned, rode on horseback in Peru and made it to the very top of the Inca trail.

"It'll soon blow over," I said a little too cheerfully, trying to control my nerves and not wanting to tell Emma that the sky was purple with storm clouds ...

I was soon given away by a loud crack of thunder.

"I'm sure it will burn off after breakfast" was all I could think of saying.

What was I going to do now? I'd been so careful in my planning of the last few months but hadn't considered that there might be a rainstorm on our tropical wedding day.

Emma

The look on Jim's face when the thunder started was awful; a mixture of disappointment and hopelessness.

This was enough to make me get out of bed and investigate for myself. However, the clap of thunder meant I didn't need to look outside to know there was a storm brewing. A few seconds later, the sound of the torrential rain on the roof was so loud that it drowned out any possibility of conversation.

Jim

"It's OK my lovely," she said as she reassuringly put her arm around me.

Wasn't it my role to comfort her? I was amazed at her calmness at accepting the situation.

"There's nothing we can do now but enjoy the day, and if it means getting wet, then so be it!" she said.

At this moment, as if I needed any further reassurance, my nerves vanished as I knew that Emma was my soul mate.

Go! Read
Life's Little Treasure Book on Marriage & Family, H Jackman
Brown

Emma

It would have been nice to get married in the sunshine, but at
least the rain meant it would be cooler and we would be alone on
the beach. We could have the blessing under the gazebo area and
not worry about getting wet.

Jim studied my face, holding his breath for my reaction. How
could I let a simple tropical storm spoil our day after all the
adventures we had been through in the last seven months? In a
way it added to the spirituality of the occasion.

Jim

"It's OK my lovely," she said as she reassuringly put her arm
around me. "Now all I need you to do is disappear while I get
ready. Why don't you go and see where they are planning to hold
the ceremony now?" Emma directed. She was clearly eager to
start getting ready in peace, so I went to find Lucy.

"Do you still want the blessing on the beach?" asked hostess
Lucy, squinting out towards the bending palm trees from under
her cupped hands looking hopefully for a slightly brighter
horizon that suggested better weather.

"Let's move it inside under the gazebo. We'll just have to
make do," I suggested. It was time to take control.

"They reckon it's good luck to have rain on your wedding
day," said Lucy, trying her best to reassure us. "We've six staff on
today, so don't worry about a thing. They're here for you."

With the monks due in from the monastery in less than an
hour we all mucked in and relocated the flower arrangements,
kneeling mats, and offerings away from the beach front where it
had been prepared for us earlier.

Emma

With Jim gone to help with the arrangements, I set about getting ready. It did not take long, surprisingly. Hair up in a clip with white orchids to hide the untidy bits and very light make up – I did not see the point as it was probably going to be washed off by the rain in minutes!

So after about 20 minutes, I went to join Jim and the army of helpers who were busy with last minute arrangements.

Jim

My heart missed a beat as Emma walked up to me. She looked stunning. Her simple elegance belied the fact she had only taken twenty minutes to get ready. I went to spruce up myself, with a growing excitement.

According to tradition, to assure a lifetime of love, an odd number of monks attend the ceremony. Just as the clouds opened again, the three orange-robed monks graced the gazebo. My nerves came back with avengeance.

Emma

There were no nerves, no second thoughts and certainly no doubts. From the depths of my soul and every part of my being, I knew that marrying Jim was what I was meant to do. It felt so right.

Jim

The 30-minute ceremony was mentally and spiritually the most rewarding thing I'd ever done. Candles were lit, fruit offerings prepared and then the rain stopped – right on cue. As instructed, we sat back on our feet. Within minutes of assuming the awkward posture, I lost all feeling in my toes. Pins and needles began as a fluttering feeling and ended as a painful throb, as I imagined losing a couple of my toes in the name of love.

Emma

About ten minutes into the ceremony, Jim started fidgeting. Not being able to look at him for fear of losing my cotton headdress in which we had been entwined, I just had to hope all was ok. I could not understand what was wrong. He soon settled though and all visions of him bolting from last minute nerves vanished.

Jim

With my feet completely numb, I could finally relax as the monks blessed us with water. The head monk mixed a wax solution with the end of the candle and placed three dots onto our foreheads with his finger, which represented Buddha, the words of Buddha and the monks who had joined our ceremony.

"Good luck for you, this is good lucky day for you," he said looking me directly in the eyes with his gentle, childlike face.

As we exchanged rings we kissed hesitatingly, in case protocol dictated this off limits. So be it. I wanted to kiss the woman that I loved.

We were Mr and Mrs Wheat at last as we shared our first drink in over two weeks with a bottle of bubbly in a toast from Lucy.

Then there was the deafening sound of firecrackers.

"It's Chinese New Year today," announced Lucy. "Let's go and check it out – you won't believe what they get up to!"

"Nothing to do with me, my love. I had no idea," I said as I pulled Em's hand towards me and kissed her.

Chinese New Year turns out to be a very important day in the Thai calendar and a particularly lucky day to embark on new ventures.

"They're celebrating the first day of the Lunar New Year. It's basically an excuse for a bender that climaxes with the full moon after 15 days," Lucy informed us. "What year is it now then?" asked Emma.

"The year of the dog."

"Really?"

"You two couldn't have picked a better day," Lucy added.

I had to agree. We couldn't, especially with Emma's deep love of dogs.

Emma

First taste of marriage

'Bad men live to eat and drink, whereas good men eat to drink and live.'

Socrates

With the monks came an air of serenity that lingered for the rest of the day, despite the firecrackers. The ceremony had a magical essence; the storm clouds meant it was a dull day, but the light from hundreds of candles, the beautiful scent from an abundance of white lilies and the vibrancy of the monks' saffron robes added a spirituality that I had never experienced. The monks' chanting echoed around the gazebo in harmony with the rhythm of the waves crashing on the shore. With the man I loved beside me, I was truly at peace.

Go! Read
Daily Advice from the Heart, Dali Lama

The days after the wedding were as blissful as the days before. A little of the spa's teaching went by the wayside as we celebrated our wedding with champagne and a bottle of chilled South African Chenin Blanc – we had learned that a little enjoyment is good for the soul. The alcohol brought Jim out in nettle sting like blotches as it was re-introduced into his system. After an early night, he spent his first day as a married man in cookery school, learning how to cook healthy, but tasty, Thai food with no complaints from me. Start as you mean to go on is my motto.

Jim

My Grandmother always said for a marriage to be a success both partners should work at it, whatever 'it' is. Em had booked us both in for a Thai cookery course. When I say 'both' I mean that *I* spent the morning slaving over a hot stove with Em joining me to sample the meal at lunch time.

I had never previously had enough time or patience, nor the inclination to cook anything from scratch but I thoroughly enjoyed myself. Despite getting the chilli and the salt mixed up, searing my thumb instead of the chicken and squeezing lemon over both, I whipped up a delicious mix of Tom Yan Kung starter and jungle curry.

"This is lovely, Mr Wheat. I could get used to this," said Emma as she popped a plump and tasty prawn into her mouth at the cooking "meet and greet". All cooks were invited to share their dishes with their partners. It felt like she was visiting her inmate husband, coming to rescue me form the confines of the kitchen.

Emma

After plenty of time on the beach and numerous massages, we left Koh Samui to spend a week in Chang Mai, which showed us another, more gentle side to Thai life. Then Jim's voice cut across my thoughts like a knife as we cruised at 15,000 feet.

"You're OK with sharks aren't you?"

"They are a necessary part of the food chain. As long as they don't come near me, I have no problem," I replied, a little puzzled at why he had raised the subject.

Jim's organisation for our time in Thailand was impressive. I had long forgiven him for his email addiction throughout our travels as it became obvious that he had put so much hard work into our itinerary. My previous visit to Bangkok had given me a taste of the colourful country that we were married in. But there was one surprise activity that Jim had managed to keep from me until after take-off from Chiang Mai. And that tactic left me with no escape. We were returning to Bangkok to experience a shark dive at the aquarium.

Jim

Chiang Mai was a cross between bustling Bangkok and laidback Samui. surrounded by health spas, organic food restaurants and night time markets. During a traipse around a night market and despite the organic options, temptation got the better of me and after a refreshing *Singa* beer I opted for a burger and fries. This was a big mistake; my system clearly wasn't ready for this and within minutes I was crouched over the bowl in the gents' loo with my fingers down my throat. It just didn't feel right having that sludge inside me. My body couldn't cope with an onslaught of processed food. Our digestive tracts had been finely tuned to accept simple, unadulterated, food.

At the night market we found a teak Buddha mural; the perfect keepsake for our time in the east. Em disappeared to look at a selection of sequinned shoes, leaving me to haggle for all I was worth. I managed to settle with just under half price by the ploy of dismissively throwing my arms up and walking away from the sale several times.

"So did you get a good price?" she asked, laden with carrier bags as she returned to the stall-holder who was busy wrapping our mural in newspaper.

"Naturally," I replied, "and what have you been buying now?" as I tried to grab one of her bags out of her grasp and take a peek.

"Just little bits and pieces," she replied as she attempted to escape to another stall. Soon enough, the Thai wrap-around trousers, sarongs, sandals and incense that she'd bought were bundled into the back of a tuk-tuk, along with our Buddha.

Back in Bangkok we faced our final challenge at the public aquarium in the Siam Paragon shopping centre. 'The Ultimate Dive with the Ultimate Predator,' takes place in a three million-litre tank in the Deep Ocean exhibit. Everything in the aquarium, from the algae to the three-metre sharks, was real. We were in at the deep end with leopard sharks, tawny nurse sharks, bamboo sharks and ragged-tooth sharks imported from Africa.

Emma

"We are meeting Robin this afternoon and he is going to run through the dive with us," Jim informed me leaning over and planting a kiss on my cheek as though what he was planning was a completely normal affair, "what to do and what not to do. There's nothing to worry about."

Robin, a friend of Jim's, was in the process of setting up a diving experience in the Bangkok aquarium amongst the sharks and rays.

I have no problems with diving, but I have a big problem with sharks. This problem goes back to my childhood when in the warm balmy, summer evenings in Devon, my brother and I would go down to Meadfoot beach and swim off the slipway at high tide. The crystal-clear water exposed a map of seaweed and sand that snaked its way out to the raft anchored within a five-minute swim offshore.

Before leaping into the icy cold water, Andrew and I would plan our route out to the raft through the avenues of swaying seaweed. I would imagine all sorts of mythical sea creatures lurking within and stick to the sandy swimming path. Andrew on the other hand, seemed fearless, and would often swim right through the middle of a large patch of bladderwrack, suddenly pretending to be attacked by a shark. I would fall for it every time and have a mad panic to swim back to the shore.

And my husband, Jim was now suggesting that I voluntarily get into a large tank with several of these creatures with no protection other than a wetsuit? A wetsuit under these circumstances is about as much use as a tissue paper umbrella in the monsoon.

Jim

"None of these sharks will attack unless seriously provoked," assured Robin. "The biggest worry you will have," he added, "is that you will have an audience, so look your best!" I wasn't convinced as a ragged-tooth shark stared right at me with piercing yellow eyes and a mouthful of needle-like teeth. The giant grouper is as intimidating a creature as any of the sharks. These huge one-metre-long mouths can swallow lobsters, turtles and even small sharks whole. The oddest-looking animals in the tank were the spotted eagle rays with faces that are almost human, gliding gracefully through the water.

It was great fun mingling with the sharks but even more fun being watched by the hordes of people walking through the tunnel that cuts through the ocean tank in a bizarre underwater catwalk. Flashbulbs popped as we swam up and over the tunnel. Diving behind glass was as much about being seen as it was about seeing the fish.

"Congratulations guys," said Robin as we removed our fins and looked down on the mass of sea life we'd just swam amongst. "You two were the first-ever tourists to dive in the tank."

"Now you tell us!" shrieked Emma. "We were the daft tourist guinea pigs that Bangkok had been waiting for."

"Well, if you can do that together I reckon you'll be married for a very long time. We had to start somewhere." He paused. "At least we know it is safe now."

Emma

It was one of the most memorable experiences of my life.

"That was amazing Robin, they were all so friendly, I didn't think that they would come so close," I exclaimed. "It's only because they haven't been fed yet this morning," he said, walking away nonchalantly.

I gawped at him open-mouthed, utterly speechless. It just proves that sometimes in order to make the most of a situation it is better to be left in ignorance.

What I had just experienced in the last half an hour and in fact in the last eight months, made me realise I was finally living my life to the full. Making the most of each opportunity and not having any regrets was going to be something that I was going to live by from now on.

Jim

From whence we came

'Don't hurry, don't worry, you're only here for a short visit,
So be sure to stop and smell the flowers. '
Walter Hagan

Thailand had been a fantastic last port of call. As we headed back to the Arabian Gulf I considered the options that had presented themselves on our travels. We had lots of memories, a bit of debt, no Air Miles left, detoxed bodies and a blank canvas on which to paint our lives together. Socrates decided that a life unexamined was not worth living and that our period of quiet time and reflection was, according to his philosophy, vital. Many people may waste their lives pursuing useless or even dangerous goals like fame, riches and pleasure without asking themselves whether these are important.

"But what next for us?" I asked my wife as she closed her journal.

"Sleep for me, I'm tired."

"Not now. I meant …well I meant our next step."

"We'll have to wait and see."

Emma

Sitting on that plane back to Dubai, I had six hours to contemplate the previous eight months and the months that lay ahead. We had taken a step into the unknown without knowing the full facts. We had experienced situations that were uncomfortable and which stretched us beyond anything I thought I would ever do. Now what?

The questions that we had taken the time to answer had guided us some way towards what we wanted to do, but as yet no opportunity had presented itself. Were we a little naive thinking that our future would fall into our laps? Shouldn't we go out and create a future for ourselves?

The answers to these questions have become our goal to what we want our lives to include. It is now up to us how we plan out the road map to get there.

With everything that we had seen, experienced and learnt about, our lives would certainly take on a different outlook no matter where we ended up; a little less wasteful, more respectful of other people and certainly healthier.

We had started on this journey as two independent people. We were now coming to the end of our travels, still as two independent people, but looking in the same direction, realising that our journey was really only just beginning. It was the starting point of gathering the knowledge, and the real challenge now is how that knowledge is to be put into action, remembering to smell the flowers along the way.

Go! Read ...And Wisdom Comes Quietly, Helen Exley
Not the end: just the end of the beginning

GO! Think
Take action from today onwards. Help yourself live your life to its full potential.

Go! Do it
GO! Smell the flowers – One journey, many discoveries.

Epilogue

'The voyage of discovery lies not in seeking new vistas but in having new eyes.'
Marcel Proust

Jim

It was not just the plane that landed in Dubai with a bump; we did too. After ten months of what felt like one endless summer holiday we were geographically back where we had started but with wedding rings, the same surname and no clear plans for the future.

Running through 6 weeks of pointless Dubai post seemed rather trivial having shed most of my possessions, ties and badges of success. I now realised just how much we had compared to some of the people we met on our travels who had left their impressions on us. As much as they had impacted us, the reality was that we simply had to earn a living again.

Several options had presented themselves to us from running the hotel in Thailand, purchasing the cottage in Franschoek, going back the U.K, Peru or France. Maybe living on a hippy commune and pass the time with group hugs, saving the world and living off the land. Why couldn't we start to have quality time right now, really listening to what we truly desired - and taking action to put the life we really wanted into effect? Over those ten months, we grew together and focused on what it was it that we *actually* wanted?

We wanted to give it another go in Dubai as we took over the old company flat and bedded down to find jobs, get visas and embark on the next stage of our exciting journey. Was it back to wrestling with materialism and the whole viscious circle again?

Emma

Why Dubai?

'Slow down and enjoy life. It's not only the scenery you miss by going too fast – you also miss the sense of where you are going and why.'
   Eddie Cantor

Before we travelled, people would say to us: "You are so lucky to be able to do that, I wish I could". Well our response to them now is this: we are not "lucky". We made it happen because it is something we both wanted. When you focus on where you want to go, the obstacles in the way are moveable. The truth is, you can find a way around most things if you really want something to happen. Have the belief in what you want to do.

So we decided to stay in Dubai?

For now, Dubai ticks all the boxes for us. The trite and tarnished way we saw the place before our travels has all but gone. We still have our moments of 'What on earth are we doing here?' and quickly remember the perspective of endless possibilities we have at our fingertips.

But not only that, it offered us a fast track steeping stone; we had an apartment waiting for us, all our worldly goods (that fitted into the spare room) and it was tax free! Ironically, the opportunity for building on our experiences was staring at us from the very place we left.

It took us both a while, even after coming back to Dubai to figure out the answers to the five questions we answered. They are constantly under review as we grow, change and discover new things.

It has given us a road map to see where we are going. Along the way, we may take a detour, but we are the ones in control, we are driving where we want to go.

What are my answers now?

1. What is my ideal day; what does it involve?
An early morning walk, looking on a world that is still secret from all other sleeping beings. Having a connection and a conversation with people that will have some sort of impact in their lives on any scale. Writing words that will either bring laughter, love or tears. To experience each day to the full.

And to go home to Jim and the dogs, snuggle up in front of the log fire, a mug of hot chocolate in hand and talk about our day and its achievements. Before falling into crisp fresh cotton sheets (you can take the comfort from the girl but you can't take it away for ever.)

2. What do I want in my life?
The material things have not really changed from the original answers, but they have become 'nice to haves' rather than necessities. However, what I have realised is that there are other things in my life that give me more satisfaction; they are my values and when I am honouring them, my life has fulfilment:

- Experiencing the full range of life
- Adventure of going to the edge
- Authenticity
- Freedom to soar
- The right to choose

3. How can I make a difference?
To help people to find their full passion for life.
To put the spotlight on others to highlight their magnificence.
To bring out the strengths and hidden treasure in people, guide them find a way to fulfil their potential and occupy that space to the max.

4. What is my true life purpose or calling?
To shine a light on the life of possibility that is waiting for each one of us.

5. When do I truly live in the moment?
After completing Reiki I & II, I try and have a quiet start to the day, healing. This is the time that I meditate and forget the past, present or future of the world around. There are also times throughout the day when I am either happy, content, sad or angry when I will stop and recognise that particular feeling. It focuses the mind to the source of the emotion and I find that there is an amazing learning from doing this. A heightened sense of self awareness to experience the moments of each day.

Jim

So what next?

Even though our flat is the same one we lived in before, it, like us, it has changed. The once cream walls are now almost tasteful shades of purple, lime green and red that overlook the busier 14 lane highway. With our beliefs, dreams and earplugs to protect us we settled back to the Dubai way of life.

It felt different this time, it wasn't through gritted teeth and our new outlook and way of life helped. Our travels had temporarily changed our daily routines including the extreme confines of the spa that added to the experience. Now that we were back in the land of fine food and drink how would we adjust apart from curling up in a ball and denouncing everything around us?

"Re-write the answers to your 5 questions" reminds Emma as I'm still pretty sure they'd be the same answers, although they weren't, exactly:

1. What is my idea day; what does it involve?

Exercise in some form, connecting with people and bouncing ideas around with Emma, with or without coffee but preferably with fresh air and laughter.

2. What do I want in my life?
I wish to become deeply fulfilled as opposed to 'well off' or 'happy'. This fulfilment can come through helping others or at least developing a meaningful connection through selflessness. It is not 'all about Jim' anymore and I am working on exercising the virtues of listening and patience and developing inner peace in myself and others. Less coffee helps.

3. How can I make a difference?
Spread my contagious enthusiasm, strive for excellence, not perfection and connect both face to face and through virtual worlds, however one chooses to define them. To remain passionate about whatever it is I am doing which will in turn inspire others to believe in themselves.

4. What is my true life purpose or calling?
This will unfold as life goes on but it is to instil a sense of belonging and purpose in other people as well as myself through inspiration. Life IS the purpose and anything that helps shapes me is worth embracing, sometimes reflectively, along the way.

5. When do I truly live in the moment?
When I still my chattering mind and savour the journey not the destination. From eating and drinking, to driving and talking I CAN be in the moment if I allow myself to be. When I am in the company of other people, including the wife and practice the virtues of patience and persistence. When I take the slow road and resist pulse raising temptations that have distracted me from my true aspirations.

Having answered these 5 questions for a second time in the

final section of our book it was time for another clear out. We gave away more old pointless clutter that we'd horded in the spare room, finding good homes for the things we no longer needed. The security guard was thrilled with the TV, which was an unexpected indulgence for him, the house girl, whose sister had the same size feet as Emma, loved getting all those shoes and the dog rescue centre, K9, was able to sell all the things we donated to help feed all of the dogs they had rescued.

Emma

'What you get by achieving your goals is not as important as what you become by achieving your goals.'
Zig Ziglar

Within 1 week of our return, I was approached by an events company to work on an urgent temporary project to organise a high-profile event.

It was quite a challenge and although the project was a great success, I knew that being part of the corporate lifestyle again, with the stress and pressure that came with event management, was not what I wanted. So, when the opportunity for a people-focused role came along with the same company, I took it.

But this was not getting me any closer to living the way I wanted in my five answers. And it was not helping me live by the values that I had identified.

And then I heard about coaching through a friend and have not looked back since. So much of what I learnt through coaching was about what I had discovered on our journey. It really felt as if I had come home.

In order to take this further, I had a major decision to make; do I stay in the safety and comfort of my job or do I step out over the ledge and commit myself fully to coaching? I had resigned once, with no plan other than to travel, so this time it was a little easier.

I was freeing up my time to follow my purpose and passion.

I now have my own life coaching practice, that focuses the spotlight on people's own magnificence. It helps others find their way of being passionately unique. It is up to me to make sure that my values are present in my life and this is how I do it.

By doing this I am making myself live my life to the full, taking no prisoners along the way, displaying opinions and beliefs with courage and showing up as the person I am - the person who made so many personal discoveries along our ten month journey.

The knowledge and discoveries that we have gathered along our journey have become part of who we are. The fasting at the spa has done wonders for our health and our approach to food. As much as we would love to say that we follow a raw diet and never waver, this is not the case!

But life is all about balance; the odd glass of wine, the occasional bar of chocolate (or two) and Jim is even 'allowed' the odd coffee when I am not looking. We try and eat healthily, but we are lovers of good food, so again it is about a balance.

And that is really what we have done as a result of our travels; put our lives in balance. We have found ways to continue smelling me flowers; there is always incense burning in our house (I am sure Jim is addicted), angel cards feature on a weekly basis and daily Reiki sessions help us to have a different perspective in a sometimes crazy self indulgent city in which we, for the time being call home.

Jim

'Tomorrow's the first day of the rest of my life – and that's true for you too. Stop looking over your shoulder and start looking forward.'
    Bob Sleelert

So with my revised answers to the 5 questions and with Emma now back at work, now what? Well it was my chance to dabble at some Marketing Consultancy work. My purpose, I decided was to help companies discover their purpose in the form of a vision statement framed neatly on the wall. Couple this with a list of values through a meaningful charter and my boxes where ticked, or so I thought.

My philosophy was to involve a broad spectrum of employees in forming the charter, not just the CEO.

Having spent five months weaving what I call 'my brand magic' as an independent marketing consultant one construction based client in particular liked the charter I'd produced. I had conducted several workshops not only with management but also with the input of the Hindu labourers and the Filipino office staff. Comparatively speaking they earn very little, but in relative terms to their home countries, it's a five-fold increase on what they could be earning.

The problem here is that as Dubai is the fastest-growing city in the world, with over 25 per cent of its residents involved in construction, the market for good business is here but holding onto ethics and decency remains a challenge. They threw up the most profound answers while the CEO threw an unexpected gauntlet down to me:

"The charter reads well, from the heart and it is great to talk the talk", Jim "but can you walk it?"

"Of course I can, this is more than just clever words and theory" I replied.

"Well prove it then. Run the company by your charter."

How could I refuse? At the time of writing I am the General Manager of the company and put into practice leading the team by these words. I am trusted to run the company with the autonomy that I thrive on and it's turning into a most rewarding experience – not only in financial terms but I now go home after putting in a day's work that actually means something.

I have upgraded a labour camp based on the premise that all office staff should be comfortable eating the same *dhal* as its labourers – me included! It's far removed from textbook corporate life because I have the opportunity to be and create the culture – all the things that pushed me away in the first place.

It has its challenges and the charter has helped me make some very difficult decisions in testing conditions as staff come and go in the dance of life.

It has had a knock on effect in all aspects of my life as I strive to be remembered as a 'Gentleman' as my previous labels and stereotypes fade away. I feel more genuine, more alive and more liberated than ever. Now I help others do the same, feeling valued and with their part to play in realizing their own genius.

Epilogue Part II - Getting there

Emma and Jim or is it Jim and Emma?

Jim's Epilogue

'May you have a strong foundation when the wind of changes shift'
Bob Dylan

Obsession

We'd sailed unchartered seas, discovered the places we once dreamt of seeing and tied the knot along the way as Emma and I became shadows, inseparable travel companions and soul mates. In 'time spent together' terms we'd achieved more in 2 years that most modern day domestic relationships achieve in 10.

"That's some adventure, you two really should write a book!" Friends told us.

So what started as posting a few travel photos on a static web page blossomed into a vehicle to share and give birth to GO! Smell the flowers as a brand, a blog and an online community originally designed to promote the book. People from Sydney to Seattle were emailing us applauding our courage for breaking away from the norm, something they'd hope to do one day.

With this adulation came a price as our flower smelling phrase became a contradiction in terms as countless hours of writing up our journals, editing and combining them along with the blog became my raison d'etre. Me, the fearless Construction hero by day and flower smeller by night as Emma pursued her ambition becoming a certified life coach as her vocation in life became even clearer. She was working towards opening a rural life coaching retreat in France complete with an open fire, an Aga, fresh air and countless muddy walks with dogs as I wanted to make a difference right here in Disneyland Dubai.

Brand Jim & Em

Dreaming of more places to see with Emma was gradually replaced with me imagining *GO! Smell the flowers* chalking up another week as a best seller, appearances on Oprah and foraging into relationship coaching to inspire other couples. I now realise how much I literally reached out at every given moment in the form of Jim & Em business cards trying to bait people to go onto the blog and post a comment. People were polite enough but busy getting on with their own precious existence, called life. Why did I need anyone else's approval as they glazed over listening to my tales of travel?

Our flower smelling reality was changing with me choosing to write another blog article, finalise our logo and 'one journey – many discoveries' tagline or amuse my virtual Facebook friends rather than join my wife in bed. We wanted the same things in life – didn't we? That's what all our friends, family and our soon to be publisher believed and on the surface so did we.

"Are you coming to bed yet?" Em would often ask as I tip-tapped away with my pearls of wisdom on the blog.

"I'll be in 10" I'd grunted, eyes intently locked into the laptop screen connecting online at will.

"Ten real minutes or laptop minutes" came the reply as I poked strangers, played scrabble and made virtual friends I never knew I never had.

Our virtual brand quickly justified and became the reason for being married. What we'd done and where we'd been and how I got wonderfully swept away with the whole thing without really considering the implications of real day to day life. The flowers website and book gave me the recognition and approval I craved to rubber stamp our marriage. Word spread in Dubai with appearances in local magazines, a double paged feature in a popular daily, an appearance on breakfast T.V and motivational talks to corporate ranks in Dubai. "GO! Smell the flowers" while you still can, I'd say, often all too smugly I suspect.

Showing the strain

Our marriage was beginning to suffer as I slipped into a comfort zone and into a place that was too lazy to even make love to my wife.

"Maybe it's a medical thing, babe or is it me?" An under-standably neglected Emma suggested.

"I'm fine, just a lot going on monksie moo" I'd reply defen-sively using my patronising pet name for her as a term of endearment more suited to a relationships between siblings.

Night after night was the same drill – a quick catch up, dinner, book and blog to be repeated with endless enthusiasm as the bubble of my ignorance grew. Occasionally we'd flick through the black and white wedding album, hang pictures up we'd collected on our travels and fondly look back on that precious time we had spent together. It did make great dinner conversation with friends but tended to become the theme of the whole evening. "Maybe we should buy ourselves a T.V?" I suggested after a fair observation by Em that all I ranted on about was *GO! Smell the flowers*.

Even after candlelit dinners my lack of libido would raise its head (ahem) and it was time I confronted my fear of impotency. With minimal sex drive and a lack of desire to devour my wife it was time to face the music and see a Doctor. Having blood taken to measure testosterone, hormones and cholesterol was the least I could do. The Doc confirmed it was "All perfectly normal" with, if anything, high levels of testosterone and a man to man chat hinting that it could be a simple issue with the marriage. A 7 year itch perhaps – we'd barely been married for 7 months. Let's not go there I thought and proceed to tell the Doctor about our wonderful travels, book and of course, the website.

'Look if there is anyone else you will tell me, won't you?' A question I often heard from Emma as her feelings of rejection grew. My obsession and vision became unfaithful to the flower smelling cause and our marriage.

The months passed with ground hog day recurrence with me on the site whilst Emma researched her plans of setting up the coaching retreat in France with country walks and dogs at her side. Often she'd grab my arm to look at her laptop screen with 'Look babe – I've found our dream place in France' I just couldn't get excited about it and she was beginning to suspect it. She'd found her calling and I was proud to have been a part of that but something was wrong. I went along with it with occasional grunts of approval but little more than that and was beginning to tread on dreams and feel like I was holding her back.

I was starting to resent the thought being holed up in outback France waiting for visitors to pitch up and smell the flowers with us. I wasn't ready to put my feet up by the fire, throw my head back and philosophise over life – maybe one day but not just yet. In Dubai aside from writing and the website we'd try to rekindle our pre-travel feeling with weekends away, meals out, Reiki courses, crystal healing, coaching courses and desert adventures. Inspired by the film 'The Secret', we designed dream boards – corkboard mounted scrapbooks of the future, rebelliously cutting out images and words out of magazines and books, stuff that we could attract into our lives for our respective futures.

"Let's do separate ones and compare them afterwards" I suggested only to delay the exercise and tip-tap away on the blog inspiring someone I'd never met pushing aside thoughts of France. It transpired our dream boards weren't that different with magazine clippings of the countryside, snow capped mountains, open fires, golf courses and a table with plenty of people sat around featuring on both. Were they a glimpse of the future or a scrap book of the past I wondered?

Whatever our plans for the future they started feeling conditional, full of compromise that is a given with the sacrifice of marriage and a compromise that was losing its appeal.

The desire for a legacy

I ploughed on with my life balance dangerously tipping more towards flowers than my full time job in Construction. As the website hits grew so did further career opportunities as I was headhunted and landed an 'even bigger and better job' as the construction boom in Dubai marched on.

Between jobs I was blessed again with an extended period of gardening leave meaning we could celebrate Em's fortieth birthday on the road again. Time for more travel and not even the foothills of the Canadian Rockies, salsa dancing in Cuba and another spell in a Thai spa could cover up the fact that we had different ideas for the future as we continued to run away from reality, from life.

With the 'Flowers' manuscript well and truly finished, complete with the post travel happy ending, we used the time to approach publishers and starting making inroads with agents. Em passed her certified life coaching qualification with flying colours and headed off to assist on a coaching course in Paris. I joined the boys for a golf trip and caught up with friends back in the North West of England. Most of whom were now purposeful fathers who took great exhausted pride in introducing me to their kids. It hit me that I'd like to be a Dad one day and it was never anything Emma and I had really discussed, largely as I was the child in the marriage – she already had one in the form of me! Spending time as an observer in chaotic child infested houses made me realise what was missing in my life. Children. It was something Em and I had discussed; neither of us had been keen but decided that we would cross that bridge when it appeared.

A tough call

It clicked that I wanted more – a living legacy and not the four legged variety. GO! Smell the flowers became the void filler and the chance of Emma and I leaving a legacy, the legacy you're reading now that will always be a privileged part of me. A father in my forties suddenly jumped to number 1 of my wish list and that harsh realisation led me to dig deep and follow some of my own advice.

I was starting to resent the thought of France, of not having a family around me and it was unfair to expect Emma to compromise her dreams for mine. Reflecting on some of the messages in this book such as life isn't a dress rehearsal, smell the flowers while you still can and take that leap of faith still resonated with me but I was in danger of becoming a fraud, as was the marriage.

I simply couldn't go through with house hunting in France as the whole idea turned my stomach as did the thought of not having a family in the future. Emma needed to know as we were on a collision course that would have denied us living our dreams and smelling our flowers.

Em's holiday in Amsterdam with a girlfriend was cut when I called her confirming I just couldn't go through with it. France or the marriage.

It was time to separate from my soul mate and let her fly free. I just knew it as the lights in the room of our collective vision and plans for the future faded more day by day.

We met in a Hotel in London and I, strangely determined not to show any emotion, confirmed to the woman that I swept away, shared my travel dreams with and planned to grow old with was now redundant in my life plans. This was the reality and not the discovery I'd ever planned to make but it was the truth, we were starting to head down different paths and the compromise of marriage wasn't going to help the issue.

What happened in London remains pretty much a blank, tube ride, a stale smelling hotel room with the 2008 Olympic swimming on, a Diana book gift for Emma and a tourmaline crystal from her to me. Lots of tears, tissues and the hopelessly looking dog-eared travel case of my loved one.

Everything was incidental - it had to be as it may have

stopped me carrying through my message to Emma without emotion. My form of self defence worked as I remember very little of it except that as I left having wiped a tear off Em's cheek with my clumsy thumb the heavens opened – a torrential pour down that started to wash away my feelings of abandoning my marriage. The tube ride back to my brother's served to help me contemplate focus on breathing and wondering if Emma would make it through the night and little else.

We agreed to meet back in the Dubai flat after a month apart and not contact each other at all as I entered the most isolated and emotionally draining period of my life to date. Emma retreated to her friends and family in Devon and me to mine in Chester where I started the divorce ball rolling through the UK system and the *GO! Smell the flowers* blog entries relentlessly continued.

Cards on the table

Back in Dubai after a surreal month of no contact and with no going back we agreed to press on and work on a settlement.

"What about the book and the website?" I asked.

"We've gone too far with that not to stop" came Em's stoic reply.

She still wanted it to work despite it being the saboteur of our marriage. Determined not to involve lawyers we took a leaf out of our own book and with the help of a harmony angel card on the table, between sobs and tears, completed the petition to file for divorce.

The flat was eerily how we'd left it - wedding photos, travel pictures and my favourite black and white photo of a 5 year old Emma. She was innocently holding her hand out feeding pigeons in Trafalgar square with her brother. The perfect face of sympathy, hope and giving that still brings me to tears as I type these words. The little girl I'd abandoned – how could I?

I had to and I didn't belong in the flat anymore – it was time to move on.

Em always complimented me on my 'generosity of spirit' and neither of us had expected the thorns to develop around the flowers so quickly. I didn't have the energy or desire to pack away my shelves of worthless self help books – who was I to give advice with my current life as it is with my 'one journey many discoveries?' The 'stuff' side of our partnership could wait until we were straight about our own individual futures.

Bouts of navel gazing where my way of dealing with it as our respective friends and family advised us in terms of what they thought was best for us.

"You'll need a decent lawyer and don't be too soft"

"You are sure, aren't you?"

"WHAT? You've only just got married!"

"So much for smelling the flowers! Coffee more like."

Was this really happening to us? Our friends would ask us as we gravitated to those who'd listen. This was the biggest challenge we'd had to face together – getting through this separation intact with our dignity, pride, respect for each other with as little fuss as possible.

As we adjust to living apart with our divorce now formalised with minimal fuss, no legal action and mutual respect back in Domestic Dubai. Neither of us had the headspace or the inclination to argue over the petty material stuff that is just stuff. I boxed up a couple of pictures which, it transpired, Emma never really liked (she always did has great taste) and the books I came into the marriage with.

A new start

Pulling away from Emma was an all or nothing and I needed the space to heal and decided to spend my last month of gardening leave alone in an Ashram in India and the foothills of the Himalayas. As I tip-tap away here in the foothills of Dhramashala in the midst of the loneliest period in my life I'm hopeful for the future. A new focus with a new job, the 'GO!

Smell' machine relentlessly pressing on and thought of Emma finding her feet and healing.

My appetite, energy and zest for life are slowly returning as I reflect back on how fortunate we were to do the wonderful things we did. The appeal of digging deeper and finding myself in this often heartless world continues. After my time here in India, overdosing on 'Vitamin me', I'm preparing to hustle up, to get on with living life back in Dubai and at the sharp end of a recession-filled industry as a global credit crunch has just given the world a reality check. I'd have to find somewhere to live within the next couple of weeks, prepare for the new job and get back amongst it.

The Jim & Em cocoon of comfort that became self centred and obsessed was a wonderful time. Our bubble of blissful ignorance gave us the freedom to freewheel in Provence, flush out in Thailand, Bungee in South Africa, Dart around Devon and marry in Thailand during this wonderful period of change and self discovery. Well worn trekking boots, stamp littered passports and a bag full of mixed currency had served us well and we'd served each other well, on the road. In that context, in that time we were made for each other, right for each other and complimented each other wonderfully well.

As aspects of my life withered the GO! Smell the flowers website continued to flourish with the global community becoming far deeper featuring the stories and daily sound bite of flower smellers all over the world. As it was before Facebook and twitter became so popular it was some feat that traffic was up to 50,000 hits per month. Just rewards for my obsession was an opportunity to link up with an online florist with the 'Send flowers now, why wait until the funeral?' tagline. This came at a price that almost cost me the website, friends and a $50, 000 legal case.

Although a crisis at the time it was small pickings compared to what followed during a period of deep loss in my life losing my job on three occasions since 2008 and my father, Graham in

October 2009. I really was smelling the coffee now with this wake up call and am currently writing GO! Smell the Coffee, filled with many more journeys and discoveries as the dance of life thankfully continues.

I continue to learn many lessons – lessons from life as I busy myself, keep smiling and smelling my flowers along the way wherever I may tread. Since the times of loss the opportunities that I've been blessed with reignited my zest for life in ways I'd never dreamt possible through a new career and a passion through a skill I didn't even know I had. That, as they say, is another story!

Jim dedicates this book to the memory of his late father Graham Scott Wheat, to his Mum for staying so strong and to his new wonderful nephew Hudson Graham Wheat.
Feel free to contact Jim on twitter: @flowersmeller or jim.wheat@gmail.com

Emma's Epilogue

Why Dubai?

'Life is under no obligation to give us what we expect.'
  Margaret Mitchell

Throughout out the time of settling back in Dubai, it became clear that all was not well in paradise. And what exactly was wrong – I had no idea, just a gut feeling that this once idyllic relationship now did not feel right. As I approached my fortieth year, I realised I had already made so many changes through coaching and taking a nine months' Leadership course. I was beginning to have the courage to look at what my heart really yearned for and there was a nagging fear that was it was not what Jim wanted.

He would make the right noises and tell me what I wanted to hear, but my intuition was telling me that there was much sadness ahead.

Jim resigned from his job, which meant that we had another opportunity to travel, this time for six months. I was hoping that this would bridge the growing gap that had started to appear between us, in both goals, emotional intimacy as well as physical intimacy.

This was my fortieth year and one I felt I had to start really living life, continue to build on the changes that had been made and have the courage to move towards my goals.

Our planned travels took us to Thailand, back to the spa, Canada for a ranch holiday, Cuba to discover the unknown and back to the UK to spend time with our families. It was a wonderful time of reconnection and starting to get back to how our relationship had been during the first round of travelling. Jim spent time on a boys' golfing holiday, I went to Amsterdam with a girlfriend to push the limits of my sheltered world and legally smoke some pot. We had a mortgage in place ready to find the perfect French property in August and start building the future in Europe. I felt that I was finding my balance again and was excited about the future.

And it was in Amsterdam when my world changed beyond all expectations, shattering my dreams of the future. Never did I think that my world would fall apart in a phone call.

'Sometimes the heart sees what is invisible to the eye. '
H. Jackson Brown, Jr.

As the phone rang, I saw it was Jim and was thrilled as we had missed each other's calls for a couple of days. As soon as I heard his voice, I knew something was wrong. He sounded lost, afraid and very sad.

'How's Amsterdam Em?' came his subdued voice.

'I would rather hear how you are, what is wrong you sound awful' I coaxed, knowing that reporting my love of the city and the fun we had been having would be inappropriate at this moment.

'Well I have been thinking ... I can't do France,' came the reply followed by silence.

'That's OK Jim. If it is not France then we will go somewhere else, This is something we can talk about, as long as we are together the place is not important, it is more about us being together to create what we want' I said, with an uneasy fear gripping my heart.

'Its more than that Em, I have realised that I want a family. I want to be a father figure.'

Again the silence as the fear increased its hold on my heart and started to spread to the rest of my body.

Having a family was something we had discussed at length and decided it was not for us. And if either of us had a change of heart, then we had made a pact to discuss it and cross any necessary bridges.

'And we can talk about that too,' was all I could think to say, hearing the desperation in my voice.

'No, it's more than that. Our paths in life our heading in different directions and I don't see how we can continue.'

As I heard those words, the fear seemed to squeeze every last ounce of air from my lungs. My brain refused to fully comprehend what was being said. How could this be? Was this Jim talking? Was this the person who only three weeks ago had told me how excited he was at the path we were following together? My brain, wanting to now comprehend what was going on made my mouth seek clarification before I could stop it.

'So what are you saying? Are you saying that you don't want to be married anymore?'

As soon as the words were out of my mouth I wanted to take them back. They were words I never wanted to ever hear. Maybe if I kept quiet, Jim would forget what he said and in five minutes everything would be back to normal.

But Pandora's box had been opened wide and there was no getting the lid back on.

The silence seemed to be deafening, with the only sound being my heart beating in my ears. My breath had stopped in the desperate hope that time would stop and Jim's answer would never be heard. But it came like a piercing arrow.

'Yes, that is what I am saying.'

More silence.

What followed then is a blur of emotions. Words did not make any difference.

We were to meet in London in 48 hours to have a frank and honest discussion about our future. And yet how could we have a future? Jim sounded so sure in what he wanted and I was not part of that picture.

'A real friend is one who walks in when the rest of the world walks out.'

Anon.

During those 48 hours, I searched my soul long and hard. Friends who lived in Amsterdam and the girlfriend I was with, gently held me and let me be in the space of sorrow. All the questions I was asking myself could not be answered without seeing Jim and talking this through further.

There was one question that I could answer though ...did I truly love him? That all consuming love that comes along once in a life-time? No, I think that our love had shifted to something that no longer lifted us up and let us fly side by side. Jim was right, we were on different paths that were taking us further apart and neither of us had the courage to acknowledge it ... until now.

Was I prepared to have children to save my marriage, was one of the burning questions spinning around my brain. Did I love Jim enough to make what I felt was a big sacrifice? And was this really the main reason or just a cover for something else. How could this have come as such a shock to me? Why did I not see this coming?

As I walked around Amsterdam in a daze, and waited for the water taxi I sat on the dock, staring at a high wall full of graffiti. As my brain started to register that it was all in Dutch and I could not understand it, I saw something that shocked me to my core.

There is 30 cm high, vibrant red letters, one solitary phrase written in English that I will never forget. To me it was a sign, message, and an answer. Whatever you want to call it.

'She walks away with dignity, a testament to her vulnerability.'

That moment, something deep within me knew that the marriage was over. The wonderful three years we had spent together was all that was left. There would be no more. I had to let it go.

'If you love somebody, let them go. If they return, they were always yours. If they don't, they never were.'
Anon.

And that is what I have done. I truly believe that there is no point in trying to be with someone if they don't want to be with you. I want to feel loved and cherished and be the sun in someone's universe, their reason for being and the sparkle behind their smile. I would not have this with Jim if I convinced him to stay. I knew I had to let go. Meeting him in London, it became clear that he had made up his mind that the marriage was over. There was no dilemma in whether I would have children to save the marriage – this was not an option. He wanted children and not with me.

Over the next few months of piecing myself back together, I was blessed enough to be safely wrapped up in the unconditional love of friends and family. No one trying to fix the problem, but really listening to me and letting me feel the pain and face it. To explore all the dark places so that they would not be so fearsome in the future. And for that love, space and patience, I will be forever grateful. Having the capacity to feel that love for friends in the midst of heartbreak was a true gift that showed me I was capable of loving deeply.

During this time, I have been on a roller coaster of emotions; grief, anger, acceptance and indifference.

'Anger makes you smaller, while forgiveness forces you to grow beyond what you were.'
Cherie Carter-Scott

Once the grief of what I lost passed, I got angry. How dare he make this decision and assume that I would accept it? How dare he not discuss this with me so that we could work through this to whatever conclusion was necessary? Who was he to side-line me and make me feel so helpless and irrelevant. How dare he tell me over the telephone. In fact, HOW DARE HE?

And now I recognise that it took much courage for Jim to step forward and say what he truly wanted and what he did not. I will always thank him for that courage.

Life is a work in progress and worth indulging in with all your senses intact.

What does matter is that we woke up to the importance of counting our blessings and living for the moment. Taking the decision to each follow our own paths separately is another way of smelling the flowers. Living life from the heart.

'Trust in the unknown, for it knows what you do not know......'

Leanne Shulman

The pain was like nothing I had felt before, and like the fire that destroys the phoenix it also brings strength and new life. A clay pot has to go into the kiln to become stronger and transform the glaze.

It has made me clear on what is really important. Life is too short not to consciously creating the life you want. It is too short not to speak the truth that is your heart. Life is too short to wait for circumstances to stimulate action.

Smelling my flowers now means enjoying life's simple pleasures – discovering new places, walking to the beach at dawn, allowing my heart to love fully, hearing music that moves me to tears, having a belly laugh with my friends. Courage to always make space for what is important in life.

Reality is now. Enjoying each moment and being open to all the opportunities and possibilities that present themselves. This has been a journey of many discoveries. Joyful, exciting, painful and full of the whole range of emotions. It has freed my spirit and allowed me to stand tall in who I am and want to become. It is a journey of awakening.

And I know that I will find a love that will make my heart sing and my soul soar. For that is what I know I want in my life and what makes me fully alive.

Dedicated to my beautiful mother. She is a wonderful gift to the world. And to my very dear friends who have pieced me back together. You know who you are.

Taken from The Prophet, Khalil Gibran:

And what of marriage master?
And he answers saying:
You were born together, and together you shall be for evermore.
You shall be together when the white wings of death scatter your days.
Aye, you shall be together even in the silent memory of God.
But let there be spaces in your togetherness.
And let the winds of the heavens dance between you,
Love one another, but make not a bond of love;
Let it rather be a moving sea between the shores of your souls.
Fill each others' cup but drink not from one cup.
Give one another of your bread but eat not from the same loaf.
Sing and dance together and be joyous, but let each one of you be alone.
Even as the strings of a lute are alone, though they quiver with the same music.
Give your hearts, but not into each other's keeping.
For only the hand of life can contain your hearts.
And stand together yet not too near together:

For the pillars of the temple stand apart,

And the oak tree and the cypress grow not in each other's shadow.

Our time out gave us the space to assess our lives and really focus on what we wanted in the future. Our perceptions changed along with our attitude and we now make the most of our immediate environment and the time we have. Taking time out to go and travel may not be what you want or are able to do, but whatever it is you do want, make sure you don't wait until something shocks you into doing it.

Life is a work in progress and worth indulging in with all your senses intact.

We are all writing the story of our life, everyday and our book has gone some way to helping understand what role we play! We broke away, we were 'different'.

So GO! Smell the flowers before you are pushing them up.

BOOKS

O is a symbol of the world, of oneness and unity. In different cultures it also means the "eye," symbolizing knowledge and insight. We aim to publish books that are accessible, constructive and that challenge accepted opinion, both that of academia and the "moral majority."

Our books are available in all good English language bookstores worldwide. If you don't see the book on the shelves ask the bookstore to order it for you, quoting the ISBN number and title. Alternatively you can order online (all major online retail sites carry our titles) or contact the distributor in the relevant country, listed on the copyright page.

See our website **www.o-books.net** for a full list of over 500 titles, growing by 100 a year.

And tune in to myspiritradio.com for our book review radio show, hosted by June-Elleni Laine, where you can listen to the authors discussing their books.

MySpiritRadio